A SYSTEM
OF NEWBORN
PHYSICAL
EXAMINATION

A SYSTEM OF NEWBORN PHYSICAL EXAMINATION

by
John W. Scanlon, M.D.
Thomas Nelson, M.D.
Lawrence J. Grylack, M.D.
Yolande F. Smith, M.D.

From the Division of Neonatology
Columbia Hospital for Women
Washington, D.C.
and
The Department of Pediatrics
Georgetown University School of Medicine

University Park Press
Baltimore

UNIVERSITY PARK PRESS
International Publishers in Science, Medicine, and Education
300 North Charles Street
Baltimore, Maryland 21201

Copyright © 1979 by University Park Press
Second printing, September 1981

Typeset by American Graphic Arts Corporation.
Manufactured in the United States of America by The Maple Press Company.

Library of Congress Cataloging in Publication Data
Main entry under title:

A system of newborn physical examination.

Bibliography: p.
Includes index.
1. Infants (Newborn)—Medical examinations.
I. Scanlon, John W.
RJ253.S87   618.9'201   78-31255
ISBN 0-8391-1392-7

Contents

Contents

Authors

John W. Scanlon, M.D.
Director of Neonatology
Columbia Hospital for
Women*
2425 L Street, N.W.
Washington, D.C. 20037;
Associate Professor of
Pediatrics
Georgetown University
School of Medicine
Washington, D.C. 20007

Thomas Nelson, M.D.
Neonatologist
Columbia Hospital for
Women
Assistant Professor of
Pediatrics
Georgetown University
School of Medicine

Lawrence J. Grylack, M.D.
Neonatologist
Columbia Hospital for
Women
Assistant Professor of
Pediatrics
Georgetown University
School of Medicine

Yolande F. Smith, M.D.
Neonatologist
Georgetown University
Hospital
Instructor of Pediatrics
Georgetown University
School of Medicine

---

* Mailing address.

Acknowledgments

The authors express their appreciation to Mrs. Dolores Sanders for her secretarial assistance and to Ms. Jan Lewis for her help with Figure 8-1.

Dedication

The authors dedicate this book to the many newborns who have been given to us for care. These tiny patients have rewarded our efforts by teaching us the substance of this text. To them we are deeply indebted.

My mother groaned! My father wept.
Into the dangerous world I leapt:
Helpless, naked, piping loud:
Like a fiend hid in a cloud.

William Blake
(1757–1827)
Songs of Experience,
"Infant Sorrow"

A SYSTEM
OF NEWBORN
PHYSICAL
EXAMINATION

1 / INTRODUCTION AND OVERVIEW

The authors have been teaching physical examination of the newborn to medical students, pediatric residents, and nurses for a number of years. We have developed a system that we think the beginning student of neonatology will find helpful. Such a system is, of course, idiosyncratic. There are any number of ways to approach the newborn's physical examination. Experienced neonatal practioners may not agree with our system; however, experience has taught us that it works.

For convenience and in order to provide the student with a systematic framework in which to perform the exam, in this text, the newborn's physical findings are arbitrarily categorized under certain organ systems. However, it must be remembered that there are an infinite number of potential interactions between organ functions in the human. Thus, peculiar findings under one heading may well denote abnormality in one or more other systems.

One of the most important parts of neonatal physical diagnosis, perinatal history, is not covered in this book. It must be emphasized that the history of the newborn is as important in arriving at a correct diagnosis as physical characteristics or laboratory findings. The newborn is only newly born. He has a history extending back to the time of conception. He has been influenced by events that impinged upon his parents even before that time.

In one sense, the newborn physical examination represents a screening procedure. If historical antecedents suggest the likelihood of pathology in a specific organ system, necessarily the examination of that system will be more detailed, more focused, and more exhaustive. As one simple example, a maternal history of diabetes mellitus argues for close observation to detect hypoglycemia, jaundice, respiratory distress, or other serious problems. Such a history also suggests that careful observations of the sacrum and perineum be carried out. Specific neurological testing of the anal wink reflex as well as of lower extremity sensory and motor function should be done, since there is an increased incidence of congenital caudal-sacral abnormalities in offspring of diabetic women.

This brings us to a second concept intrinsic to physical diagnosis of the newborn: The more expanded the student's knowledge of perinatal medicine, the more efficient and precise will be the physical examination. In simplified terms, it is frequently a wonder to medical students how an experienced pediatrician can satisfactorily complete a routine examination in 8 to 10 minutes. Yet, with practice, clinical experience, and continued education, such expertise is readily achieved.

In this book we generally emphasize a "how to" approach; however, there are some guidelines and caveats to be emphasized. First among these is that observation is a most important aspect of neonatal physical diagnosis. The critical eye will discern unusual skin color, peculiar facial physiognomy, abnormal or asymmetrical motor activity, and unusual lumps, bumps, and the like. Observation by ear will also detect nuances in cry pattern, pitch, and tone of clinical salience. As an example, it has been demonstrated that the cry of the term asphyxiated newborn is shorter, its range in pitch is greater, and there is much more vibrato (Sirvio and Michelsson, 1976). An experienced ear will hear these differences. Such non-invasive maneuvers pay enormous dividends to the careful observer. The student should spend as much time as necessary prior to palpation, percussion, or auscultation looking at the infant. Note how the baby moves, breathes, and responds to extraneous sounds. Look at his fingers and toes, face, ears, lower back, abdomen, and chest. Regard his skin color carefully, and note rashes and peeling. Ask yourself, is the baby comfortable and healthy-looking? Or, is he distressed or unusual in appearance? Close observation and an intuitive sense will reward you by heightening awareness to subtle clues portending potentially serious problems. When possible, observe the infant interacting with his mother (or other caregiver) in order to gain even more information about neurological behavior, feeding ability, the autonomic nervous system, and neurological control.

Another hint is that the examiner should disturb the infant as little as possible, particularly at the start of the examination. Defensive responses to cold stress, excessive handling, and other noxious stimuli will change the infant's activity, his vital signs, and his behavior. Another word of caution: keep as much of the infant covered as possible. Remember how diaper and shirt came off when you remove them. Both baby and nurse will appreciate your replacing these garments.

The parts of the examination that are most easily obscured by the crying infant should logically be performed first. The following outline is suggested as a reasonable, albeit idiosyncratic, approach to the newborn examination once you have mastered individual components of each system.

1.   Observe the respiratory rate and the ease of respiration before disturbing the infant. Note his color at rest.
2.   Listen to the easily exposed parts of the chest for heart rate and transmitted murmurs.

3. Gently unclothe the chest, loosen the diaper, and turn the infant to the supine position.
4. Listen to the rest of the chest for murmurs and heart and breath sounds.
5. Palpate the abdomen.
6. Perform those parts of the eye exam requiring an ophthalmoscope.
7. If the infant is still quiet, or at least consolable, measure his blood pressure.
8. Neurological and behavioral observation can be done at this point.
9. Make an orderly progression, head to toe, testing those parts of organ systems contained within the region of the longitudinal axis you happen to be in. For the most part, it is immaterial at this point whether the baby is crying.
10. Measure the baby's weight, length, head circumference, and perhaps chest circumference.
11. Recheck the baby's sex. Parental rapport will vanish if you say "she" is a "he," or vice versa.

Quantitive data are collected both at the beginning and the end of the exam so that these values may be written down and not forgotten. During the course of the examination you should concentrate on remembering only those findings that are abnormal. If this is done, you may proceed rapidly through an extensive examination and end with a small number of relevant observations that must be remembered.

In special situations where extensive abnormalities are present, our method breaks down, and you may have to revert to the tedious but safe approach of examining and recording all the components of the baby's organ system as a unit.

To reiterate, no matter how the physical examination was performed, it is always important to review the findings system by system in one's mind before recording the results in order to be sure that nothing has been omitted.

Finally, it should be remembered that one of the most important prognostic and diagnostic techniques is to repeat evaluations over time, no matter what you are looking for. The infant who shows improvement in function is clearly more optimistically regarded than one who does not. This is particularly true for neurological and behavioral characteristics, but it holds for all other characteristics as well. Should you discover a finding that is troublesome, repeat your examination later. Carefully record your observations in writing. A dynamic record provides invaluable information that has both immediate and long-term significance.

You cannot learn physical diagnosis from a book. You must practice your skills repeatedly to gain competence and confidence. You will soon have the privilege and responsibility of examing a new human life. We hope that the system to be described provides guidance for you.

LITERATURE CITED

Sirvio, P., and K. Michelsson. 1976. Sound-spectographic cry analysis of normal and abnormal newborn infants. Folia Phoniatr. 28:161.

2 / GESTATIONAL AGE ASSESSMENT

Estimation of whether a newborn is premature, at full term, or post-mature is the single most important variable in clinical diagnosis. The premature newborn suffers certain serious problems, such as hyaline membrane disease, asphyxia, and necrotizing enterocolitis, much more frequently than does the full-term infant; post-mature infants have their own special difficulties. While certain historical information from the pregnancy may be helpful in estimating gestational age before delivery, the mother's estimates of such dates are often inaccurate, and other obstetrical information is highly variable. Neonatal weight, length, and head circumference relationships are important to the clinician as indicators of intrauterine growth and development. Because these relationships must be based on an accurate and precise measure of gestational age to be of maximal value, several methods have been developed to assess newborn maturity. These methods are based on external physical characteristics and/or neuromuscular function.

The scoring system most widely used is one described by Dubowitz, Dubowitz, and Goldberger (Dubowitz, Dubowitz, and Goldberger, 1970) in which eleven physical characteristics, observable in the first 24 hours after birth, are scaled from 0 to 4. This *external characteristic* score, as a summation, provides a reliable and immediate estimate of gestational age. Dubowitz et al. also described ten *neuromuscular* findings, including passive and active ranges of extremity motion, muscle tone, several spinal reflexes, and resting posture, and scored them with a similar range. These measures are carried out after the first days of life, when the infant is quiet and has recovered from any intrapartum stress. While physical characteristics and neuromuscular findings themselves are each predictive of gestational age, the sum of both scores is even more accurate. It should be noted that, even performed by the best examiners under the best conditions, this clinical estimation of gestational age is accurate only to plus or minus 2 weeks.

For certain high-risk infants (such as newborns admitted to the intensive care nursery), the Dubowitz system is preferred. For most clinical purposes, however, particularly in a regular nursery, a more rapid assessment of gestational age is practical.

The following external characteristics are most useful in this assessment: breast size and nipple formation, skin texture and opacity, ear cartilage formation and firmness, plantar skin creases, and hair distribution and texture. A rough estimate of maturity based on these criteria may be obtained by using the guidelines described in Table 2-1.

Nicolopoulos et al. (Nicolopoulos et al., 1970) have provided a simplified neurological assessment based on the Dubowitz examination. They note eight neurological criteria that have a high, statistically significant correlation with gestational age. These criteria are described in Table 2-2, along with how they change with increasing gestational age. Since performing these maneuvers requires experience, we describe in some detail how they are done.

Posture   The infant must be supine and quiet. Observations are made for arm, hip, and knee extension and flexion.

Square Window   The hand is flexed upon the wrist. Gentle pressure is exerted to obtain as much flexion as possible. The wrist should not be rotated. The square window is that angle formed between the hypothenar eminence and the anterior forearm.

Ankle Dorsiflexion   The foot is flexed on the ankle with gentle but sufficient pressure to obtain maximum flexion. The angle between the top of the foot and the front of the leg is measured.

Popliteal Angle   The infant is laid on his back, with the pelvis flat on a firm surface. The leg is first flexed on the thigh. Then the thigh is fully flexed with one hand. The other hand is used to extend the leg until the maximal angle is obtained.

Heel To Ear Maneuver   With the infant on his back, his foot is moved as near to the ipsilateral ear as possible without exerting force. The pelvis must be kept flat on a firm surface.

Scarf Sign   Again, with the infant on his back, one of his hands is drawn across the neck, as far as possible to the contralateral shoulder. The elbow may be lifted across the baby's body.

Head Lag   The infant is still on his back. The examiner grasps each forearm just above the wrist and gently pulls the infant to a sitting position. Observations are made of the relationship between the head and the trunk as the infant is raised forward beyond 90 degrees from the bed's surface.

Ventral Suspension   The infant is laid on his abdomen, with the chest resting on the examiner's hand. Then the child is lifted perpendicularly from the examining surface. Scoring is based on the amount of caudal and cephalic muscle tone exhibited.

As in so many other aspects of the newborn physical examination, the estimation of gestational age becomes more reliable as the examiner gains experience. Indeed, the scoring system developed by Dubowitz et al. has become an invaluable quantitive clinical research tool. For most

Table 2-1. Maturity estimate using the Dubowitz system

Physical Characteristics	Gestational Age		
	Premature	Transitional	Term
Breast Tissue Nipple Formation	Below 5 mm	6–10 mm	Greater than 10 mm[a]
	No areola	Areola present but not raised	Raised above skin level
Skin Texture and Opacity	Abdominal veins clearly visible, including tributary venules	Veins and some tributaries seen	Some large veins indistinctly seen
Ear Form and Cartilage	Soft, little, or no cartilage	Antitragus cartilage, perhaps cartilage in antihelix	Firm cartilage in tragus and helix
Hair Texture and Distribution	Wooly or fuzzy, very fine hair	Silky or coarser hair	Individual strands seen
Genitalia			
Male	Scrotum empty, no rugae	Descending testes, few rugations	Testes in canal, scrotum rugated
Female	Prominent labia and clitoris	Major labia larger than minor	Clitoris and labia minora skin covered[b]
Plantar Creases	Few if any	Creases up to the anterior ⅓ of sole	Entire sole creased

[a] May have breast milk.
[b] At term, milky vaginal discharge or occasionally bleeding seen at introitus.

Table 2-2. Neurological assessment scoring

Maneuver	Gestational Age			
	Very Premature	Premature	Transitional	Term
Posture	Arm and leg extension	Slight arm, moderate leg, flexion	Legs abducted, arms flexed	Completely flexed
Square Window	90°	45–60°	30°	0°
Ankle Dorsiflexion	90°	45°–75°	20°	0°
Popliteal Angle	180°	160°–130°	110°–90°	Less than 90°
Heel to Ear Maneuver	Easily, completely, touching ear	Foot almost to face	Halfway from 90° to face	90°
Scarf Sign	Elbow to opposite axilla	Elbow beyond midline thorax	Elbow to midline	Elbow unable to reach midline
Head Lag	No head support	Little head support	Head in same plane as body briefly	Head held forward
Ventral Suspension	Complete hypotonia	Slight caudal tone	Moderate caudal, slight cephalic tone	Considerable caudal and cephalic tone

clinical purposes, the examiner should be able to decide whether a newborn is at term, transitional, premature, or very premature. These categories correspond to 38–41 weeks, 35–38 weeks, 30–35 weeks, and below 30 weeks,respectively. Such estimates can be easily made using the criteria in Tables 2-1 and 2-2.

Next we must consider the observable characteristics of the post-term infant. The examiner should remember that the post-term newborn (also described as the post-date or post-mature infant) is defined solely by gestational age; simply, a newborn who has resided in utero 42 weeks or more. In general, the neurological findings of such infants will be even more advanced than those of the at-term newborn. These infants appear very alert, bright-eyed, and well coordinated, with excellent muscle tone. They may have thick skin with many superficial creases, large breasts, long fingernails, and luxuriant hair.

Unfortunately, a high percentage of post-term newborns also suffer from intrauterine malnutrition and/or perinatal asphyxia due to placental insufficiency. Such infants have been labeled "dysmature." The post-term infant's skin may not have its covering of cheesey, greasy vernix caseosa. It is not clear whether this is, or is not, related to fetal malnutrition. In any case, the skin many easily crack or peel. If there was intrauterine malnutrition, subcutaneous tissue may be decreased, causing the baby to look scrawny. Calculating the relationship between length and weight may show the infant to be disproportionately light, further supporting a diagnosis of undernutrition. There may be meconium staining of the umbilical cord, skin, or nails, which is suggestive evidence for intrauterine asphyxial distress. Green meconium staining is of recent origin. Yellowish discoloration implies chronicity, since some time must elapse to oxidize the green meconium pigment to yellow. Finally, neurological examination may show evidence of antecedent asphyxia, such as tremors or hypotonia. The examiner must remember that such findings are evidence of pre-existent or ongoing pathology, and do not reflect the normal circumstances of the post-term neonate.

LITERATURE CITED

Dubowitz, L. V., C. Dubowitz, and C. Goldberger. 1970. Clinical assessment of gestational age in the newborn infant. J. Pediatr. 77:1–10.

Nicolopoulos, D. P., A. Perakis, M. Papadakis, D. Alexiois, and D. Aravantios. 1976. Estimation of gestational age in the neonate. Am. J. Dis. Child. 130:477–580.

3 / EVALUATION IN THE DELIVERY ROOM

This chapter provides an overview of how to approach the initial screening evaluation of the neonate in the delivery room. The examiner's concerns are whether the infant's life is in jeopardy; whether the infant has started or established his transition from fetal to neonatal life; and whether there are any serious morphological abnormalities. These questions can be answered by a cursory, but directed, delivery room examination.

Again, historical clues can alert the examiner to certain diagnostic probabilities. High-risk perinatal factors, fetal heart rate abnormalities during labor, excessive maternal medication during parturition, and the like augur that the neonate may be born asphyxiated or depressed. The clinical yardstick used in the minutes after birth to determine the extent of vital sign disruption is the screening system developed by Virginia Apgar (Apgar, 1953). The various components of the Apgar score are seen in Table 3.1.

Because the Apgar System relies heavily on measures of cardiopulmonary function, and reflex and motoric central nervous system phenomena, the infant with a low Apgar score is in serious jeopardy. Further, an Apgar score below 3 at any time means that viability is threatened unless resuscitative intervention is performed quickly. The Apgar score is a dynamic measure. It can, and should, be carried out over the entire period of delivery room stabilization. The examiner must never wait for any predetermined time interval to pass before doing the score, although convention records the scores at 1 and 5 minutes as evidence for or against acute or persistent perinatal asphyxia.

The variables measured on the Apgar score are essentially vital signs, and when impaired, signify serious homeostatic disruption. Depression of the heart rate is the single most telling observation about the state of acid-base stability. Next must be rated respiratory effort, since without substantial, repetitive, and vigorous breathing, asphyxia supervenes. Muscle tone and reflex irritability are acute measures of central nervous system integrity, which can be depressed by many serious perinatal insults, including asphyxia and maternal medication, among others. Color is least reliable. Certainly, profound or pervasive cyanosis is ominous. However, most newly born infants have blue fingers and toes (acrocyanosis.)

It should be noted that the Apgar method measures depression of vital signs. Of course, some perinatal insults may result in an increased

Table 3-1.   Components of the Apgar score

Vital Sign Measured	Score		
	0	1	2
Heart Rate	Absent	Less than 100	Above 100
Respiratory Effort	Absent	Weak or gasping	Strong, regular or crying
Muscle Tone	Absent (flaccid)	Poor; some extremity flexion	Strong; full flexion
Reflex Irritability (Nasal catheter or sole pinprick)	None	Weak or delayed	Prompt and vigorous
Color	Blue or pale	Acrocyanosis	Pink

After Apgar, 1953.

heart rate (as with infection, for example), an increase in respiratory effort (pneumonia), or an increase in muscle tone and/or reflex irritability (certain stimulant drugs). The Apgar System will not screen for these influences.

Apgar scoring is subjective, which is both a strength and a weakness. The strength lies in the Apgar's simplicity, which allows easy scorer training. Additionally, it requires little equipment, and the score can be rapidly calculated. Subjectivity is clearly a weakness, however, because it may lead to significant error. Dr. Apgar admonished, therefore, that her scoring system should be administered by an observer who is not involved in the care of either mother or newborn (Apgar and James, 1962).

The Apgar's predictive ability for subsequent neurological outcome has been over-emphasized. Although neonates with very low 5-minute Apgar scores do have statistically diminished neurological performance, 95% of surviving full-term neonates with 5-minute scores below 3 are not neurologically abnormal on follow-up examination (Drage and Berendes, 1966).

The student should recognize that the Apgar is a discontinuous scale. That is, the biological "distance" between an Apgar of 1 and 4 is quite different and larger than this same "distance of 3" between 7 and 10. When moving from 1 to 4, resuscitation has been successful in reversing a mortal insult. Traveling from 7 to 10 on the Apgar scale merely denotes shades of "normality."

Some authorities recommend aspirating the neonate's stomach immediately after birth to check for esophageal patency, and to determine if gastric residue is excessive. This finding suggests the possibility of high intestinal obstruction, but it is quite subjective. Others recommend passing catheters nasally to establish natal choanal patency. We do not routinely do this because of possible bradycardia from pharyngeal vagal reflexes. Choanal patency can be rapidly assessed by closing the baby's mouth and auscultating its nares for breath sounds. However, a history of polyhydramnios, or the observation of massive abdominal distension, does require passing a catheter down the esophagus, and determining if it lies in the stomach by insufflating air. Aspiration of gastric contents via the catheter will measure residual gastric volume. Chapter 12 discusses the abdominal exam in more detail.

There are other rapid screening maneuvers that the examiner can perform in the delivery room. Among these are the quick inspection of the infant for such gross congenital abnormalities as neural tube defects, facial clefts, abdominal malfusions, severe orthopaedic deformities, external genitourinary abnormalities, spinal anomalies or masses, anal patency, and so forth. The umbilical vessels should be checked to make sure there are two arteries and one vein. A single artery occasionally indicates other internal malformations.

It is important to note traumatic abnormalities related to the birth process itself. Such findings include asymmetrical, limited, or absent limb movement. Lack of movement of the arm may be caused by damage to the brachial plexus, resulting in the classic picture of Erb's palsy. This finding may also be associated with clavicle or humerus fracture, as well as shoulder dislocation. When Erb's palsy has been diagnosed by the characteristic lack of motion of the upper arm, or when the arm is totally flailed from damage to all components of the brachial nerve, the possibility of associated phrenic nerve injury must be entertained. Careful monitoring of diaphragmatic excursions on the side of the observed nerve damage should be undertaken. If there is any question, fluoroscopic evaluation is indicated because the paralyzed diaphragm may result in recurrent pulmonary infection. Again, when delivery has been difficult, or forceps have been used, the symmetry of smiling or grimacing should be carefully noted because of possible facial nerve paralysis.

Injury to the lower extremities is less common but does occur, particularly during breech extraction. Femoral fractures are the most serious because of the possibility of massive but occult blood loss into the femoral fascia (see Chapter 7).

The nature and distribution of any bruising or petechiae should be recorded for future reference. It should be noted that cephalohematomata are rarely seen in the delivery room, since they usually develop well after birth. Finally, dislocation of the nasal septum, a not uncommon finding, may not be related to obstetrical trauma at all, but to a congenital defect (Harkavy and Scanlon, 1978).

One special circumstance is when the amniotic fluid is meconium stained. By itself, meconium-stained amniotic fluid correlates with intrauterine asphyxia. More importantly, the aspiration of meconium by the fetus/neonate will result in a serious, frequently fatal, pulmonary disorder. Thus, the presence of meconium-stained amniotic fluid necessitates that the pharynx be cleared and the trachea suctioned under direct vision. Such a maneuver should not be performed by a neophyte.

It must be pointed out that the delivery room appraisal of the newborn is not a substitute for careful physical examinations done at a more leisurely pace in the nursery. Rather, it is a search for serious and obvious abnormalities, usually carried out because of high-risk antecedents.

As with all other neonatal physical observations, careful, accurate recording of abnormal physical findings, and how these change over time, is mandatory. This is of particular importance for the newborn's delivery room evaluation.

LITERATURE CITED

Apgar, V. 1953. A proposal for a new method of evaluation of the newborn infant. Anesth. Analg. 32:260.

Apgar, V., and L. S. James. 1962. Further observation on the newborn scoring system. Am. J. Dis. Child. 104:419.

Drage, J. S., and H. Berendes. 1966. Apgar scores and outcome of the newborn. Pediatr. Clin. North Am. 13:635.

Harkavy, K. L., and J. W. Scanlon. 1978. Nasal septal dislocation after cesarian section for breech presentation without labor. J. Pediatr. 92:162.

4 / NEUROLOGICAL EVALUATION

The central nervous system is one of the least developed of all organ systems in the human neonate. Vocal communication is limited to a primitive cry, there is little control over muscular activity, and the infant is hampered by a lack of previous experience in interpreting the input from his special sense organs.

Despite such obstacles to evaluation, the central nervous system clearly merits close scrutiny. Abnormalities observed in the newborn period may point to later problems. The brain may be abnormal in many specific genetic or developmental defects. Even a normal nervous system can be damaged by events occurring during gestation, labor and delivery, or the first months of post-natal life. As we see in this and the next chapter, however, there are techniques available for examination of specific components of the central nervous system, and the evaluation of the interaction of many of these components. The student is referred to more comprehensive works for further details (Brown, 1974; Freeman and Brann, 1977; Prechtl and Beintema, 1964; Volpe, 1975).

The traditional examination of the neonatal central nervous system may be divided into two very general parts. The first is an evaluation of those structures external to the brain, which may help to identify the baby who has a neurological disorder. The second involves systematically testing specific functions of the central nervous system.

EXTERNAL EVALUATION[1]

1. Carefully examine the head for signs of trauma.
2. Measure the head circumference, and relate it to gestational age norms.
3. Measure the size of the anterior fontanel, and palpate sutures.
4. Palpate the anterior fontanel for signs of acute intracranial volume expansion or reduction.
5. Note any dysmorphic features detected during the general physical examination. Are there any cutaneous stigmata such as an excessive number (more than six) of café-au-lait spots, or a nevus flameus involving skin innervated by the trigeminal nerve? Excessive café-au-lait spots are seen with generalized neurofibromatosis, pheochromocytoma, and tuberous sclerosis. A large nevus flameus involv-

---

[1] See Chapter 8 for further details about examining the head.

15

ing the trigeminal nerve distribution may be accompanied by intracranial vascular lesions. Many of the generalized dysmorphic syndromes carry an increased risk of abnormal brain function.

6. Are there any bruits (murmurs) audible over the skull? These are suggestive of arteriovascular malformation.

TESTING NEUROLOGICAL FUNCTION

The tests of neurological function are divided into the following sections:

a. State of alertness
b. Posture
c. Muscle tone
d. Muscle strength
e. Spontaneous and elicited muscle movements
f. Cranial nerves
g. Reflexes
h. Autonomic nervous system

State of Alertness

State of alertness (for a detailed description of state of alertness, see Table 5-1 in the next chapter) determines the way in which the infant will respond to many of the neurological evaluations. The specific states observed during the course of the neurological examination should be noted. The infant may well pass through several state changes during the examination. Persistent irritability or lethargy is not normal.

Posture

Posture refers to the position preferred by the undisturbed infant. It is largely determined by the balance of resting tonus between the groups of flexor and extensor muscles, and is clearly influenced by gestational age (Chapter 2).

The normal term newborn generally lies with his hips abducted and partially flexed, and with his knees flexed. The arms are adducted and flexed at the elbow. The fists are often clenched, with the fingers covering the thumb, but the position of the thumbs is not fixed. The spine is straight.

Abnormal Postures   Abnormal postures include persistent extension of the neck (opisthotonus), obligate flexion of the thumb, and "frog's leg" position of the hips and thighs.

Muscle Tone

The resting tension of the muscles is directly related to the infant's state of alertness, and is also influenced by his gestational age.

In the full-term newborn, muscle tone can be checked by supporting the prone infant with your hand under his chest. The neck extensors should be able to hold the head in line with body for 3 seconds. The back should be straight and the hips slightly extended. When pulled from supine to sitting position, he should maintain the head nearly in line with the body (no more than a 10° lag). With his head in the midline while supine, passive flexion and extension of the extremities should reveal nearly equal tone between arms and legs.

Below 32 weeks there is little tone, neither flexor nor extensor in the arms, legs, neck, and back. By 32 weeks there may be some flexor tone in the legs, although the arms remain in extension. Near 36 weeks there is consistent flexor tone in the legs, and less consistent flexor tone in the arms.

Abnormal Tone in the Term Newborn   Abnormal tone may mean less flexor tone in the arms than in the legs, generalized hypotonia (the infant often lies in a "frog's leg position"), or extensor hypertonus.

Muscle Strength

Muscle strength usually is directly correlated with muscle tone. However, in a few infants with neurological lesions, muscle weakness may be present in the presence of extensor hypertonus.

Muscle strength is most often evaluated with the aid of the infant's palmar grasp reflex. This reflex is elicited by the examiner's placing his index finger in the infant's palm. As the finger is pulled upward against the baby's palm, the infant's grasp tightens and his arm partially flexes. The full-term infant often has sufficient strength to support his upper body weight.

If the infant is hypotonic, the muscle groups should be inspected for loss of mass, and the appropriate joints should be checked for their range of motion (see Chapter 7).

Spontaneous Movement

All spontaneous movements, especially of the arms and legs, should be observed for their quality and symmetry. The awake (state A-2 and above) full-term infant is active, moving all limbs in an alternating fashion.

Preterm   The infant of 28 weeks or less has brief periods of spontaneous activity. He has three characteristic types of muscular activity.

At times one entire limb is moved rapidly through a large arc; at other times he may have slow, twisting movements of the extremities, neck, and spine, accompanied by grimaces. The examiner may also see occasional jerks, again of the whole limb.

By 32 weeks, symmetrical flexor movements of knees and hips are replacing the more primitive movements of the very young premature. The baby turns his head for the first time.

By 36 weeks, the flexor movements of his legs are more obvious and are no longer symmetrical.

Jitteriness   Jaw tremor is frequently seen in the vigorously crying infant. Low-amplitude tremors of arms and legs of similar frequency may be seen in a few full-term infants in state A-4 alertness. These tremors can occur following a startle, or they can be initiated by exogenous stimuli. These tremors disappear when the infant returns to state A-1.

Cranial Nerves

The cranial nerves I through XII may be tested in the newborn. Complete testing may not be necessary for all infants. History and other factors should guide the examiner in deciding to what extent testing should be done. The following responses can be found in full-term infants:

Cranial Nerve (CN)		Test
Olfactory	I	General response to oil of cloves, or very dilute aromatic solutions (ammonia, wintergreen, etc.), passed under the nose can be observed. Grimacing, eye widening, sniffing, or startle may be seen.
Optic	II	a. Turns head toward a diffuse light. Remember, however, that many nurseries are so brightly lit that the overhead lights must be turned off before this response can be elicited. (Visual fields may be tested by presenting the light at the periphery of vision.) b. Blinks in response to a flash of bright light. c. Pupils constrict in response to light. The constriction should be bilaterally equal. (This tests retina, optic nerve, and the third cranial nerve.)

Cranial Nerve (CN)		Test
		d. Wandering nystagmus should not be persistent.
(Optimal State A-2–A-3)		e. Optokinetic movement can be elicited after nystagmus. This test of cortical vision requires clear corneas and lenses plus a normal retina and optic nerve. A large cloth strip, about 6 inches wide and 18 inches long, with alternating black and white 2-inch stripes, is passed slowly back and forth about 10–12 inches in front of the baby. The eyes should follow the direction of movement. Sometimes nystagmus occurs in opposite directions.
Oculomotor, Trochlear, Abducens	III, IV, VI	a. Pupillary constriction to light is mediated by CN III.
		b. "Doll's eye"—Turning the supine infant's head to the left, and then to the right, will cause the eyes to move in the opposite direction. (CN III, IV, VI.)
		c. Persistent strabismus is not normal, although occasional disconjugate movements are seen, especially in infants in light sleep (S-1) or barely awake (A-1) states.
		d. Eyelids are observed for ptosis (CN III).
Trigeminal (Optimal State A-3–A-4)	V	a. Rooting reflex—if the cheek is touched, the infant will turn his head toward the stimulus. (Tests CN V sensory pathways.)
		b. Masseter strength may be tested by placing a finger in the infant's mouth and feeling the force of his bite.
Facial	VII	a. Facial tone is best observed in the crying infant. The angles of the mouth should not droop. With a facial palsy, the corner of the

Cranial Nerve (CN)		Test
		mouth will be pulled toward the normal side.
		b. Nasolabial creases are normally bilaterally present.
Auditory (Optimal State A-2–A-3)	VIII	a. Auditory—the infant may blink at the sound of a hand clap, or become quiet (or alter respiratory rate) when talked to. Startle response to loud sound is best in A-1 or S-1 states (see Chapter 5).
		b. Vestibular—In part tested by "doll's eye." When the head is rotated through an arc in front of the examiner, the eyes should turn in the direction of rotation. Moro's maneuver (Chapter 5) also has a vestibular mediated response to head drop.
Glosso-pharyngeal, Vagus	IX, X	a. The gag reflex should be strong, and the uvula should not deviate to one side during this reflex.
		b. The cry should not be hoarse (CN X).
Accessory	XI	a. Sternocleidomastoid function may be tested by turning the supine infant's head to the side, then observing his attempts to right it.
Hypoglossal	XII	a. Tongue strength may be tested by inserting a finger in the infant's mouth, and feeling the tongue's force as he sucks.

Reflexes

Tendon (phasic) reflexes are most easily elicited by sharp percussion with the examiner's finger over the appropriate structure. These reflexes are more brisk in the neonate than in the older child and are influenced by the infant's state. Remember, these reflexes should be symmetrical.

Reflex	Segment
Jaw jerk	CN V
Biceps jerk	Cervical 5 and 6
Knee jerk	Lumbar 2 to 4
Ankle jerk	Sacral 1 and 2

Other segments of the spinal cord may be tested with cutaneous stimulation (firm stroking with a cotton-tipped swab). For example:

Truncal incurvation reflex	A firm stroke to one side or other of the spine from neck to coccyx will cause the spine to curve in that direction. This may be used as a rough test of segmental integrity from Thoracic 2 to Sacral 1.
Anal Wink	Sacral 4 and 5. The lateral anal margin is gently stroked and muscular contraction produces the appearance of a wink (the anus constricts). (See also Chapter 12.)

Primitive Automatisms   The infant possesses a number of other reflex responses; however, few of them add to our understanding of the condition of the infant's central nervous system.

The most important of the primitive reflexes not yet discussed is the *tonic neck reflex*.

The *asymmetrical tonic neck reflex* is activated in the supine infant by turning his head to one side while restraining the body from turning. The limbs on the side toward which the infant is looking are extended, while the limbs on the opposite side are flexed. Beyond 36 weeks, when flexor tone becomes the dominant tone, the asymmetric tonic neck reflex becomes less obvious. The response of the infant may vary from time to time. It is abnormal for this response to be obligatory.

The *symmetrical tonic neck reflex* is always abnormal. It is best seen in ventral suspension where the head is in the midline and extended and the arms appear to be rigidly extended with the hands fisted.

The plantar (Babinski) reflex adds little to the evaluation of the newborn, because of continued controversy concerning the significance of the upgoing toe (Hogan and Milligan, 1971; Prechtl and Beintema, 1964).

Autonomic Nervous System

The neurological examination is not complete without some overall estimate of the adequacy of the autonomic nervous system. No new tests are needed to estimate its function. A reorganization of those pertinent observations made during the general physical examination should be sufficient for this determination.

Observations of heart rate, blood pressure, temperature, respiratory patterns, sweating, skin blood flow, peristalsis, and pupillary response to light are easy to make. All tell the examiner something about the autonomic nervous system. Of these, perhaps the most useful indices for routine analysis are body temperature, heart rate, and blood pressure. Each of these autonomically controlled functions varies in response to the central needs of the body to maintain the proper balance (homeostasis) between various organ systems. You need not record normal point values, but rather you should observe trends over time, in order to determine if this system is capable of appropriate adaptive changes in the new environment.

Local defects in the autonomic nervous system (a miotic pupil) in response to a local (brachial plexus) injury must be distinguished from generalized abnormal responses. Generalized aberrations are physical characteristics of the "sick" infant. If all functions of the autonomic nervous systems are within normal limits the infant is usually well.

Normal limits for heart rate and averages for blood pressure are given in Chapter 11. Such values are influenced by both gestational age and time since birth. Normal respiratory rates are noted in Chapter 10. A peculiar variant of the autonomic instability for vascular control is dependent lividity, described as harlequin discoloration. This is normal but disquieting to the uninitiated, since half the infant is pale and half deep red.

The deep temperature of a normal infant at any gestational age should be maintained at 37° ± 0.5°C when the child is in an appropriate thermal environment. Temperature elevations are occasionally seen in the normal newborn infant, but more often the sick infant is noted to have a low temperature or an excessive degree of temperature variation. The premature baby characteristically has a limited ability to maintain temperature homeostasis without extrinsic support.

LITERATURE CITED

Brown, J. K. 1974. General Neurology. In: F. Cockburn and C. M. Drillien (eds.), Neonatal Medicine, pp. 520–555. Blackwell Scientific Publications, Oxford.

Freeman, J. M., and A. W. Brann. 1977. Central Nervous System Disturbances. In: Richard E. Behrman (ed.), Neonatal-Perinatal Medicine, pp. 787–836. C. V. Mosby Company, St. Louis.

Hogan, G. R., and J. E. Milligan. 1971. The Plantar reflex of the newborn. N. Engl. J. Med. 285:520–523.

Prechtl, H., and D. Beintema. 1964. The Neurological examination of the full-term newborn infant. In: Spastics Society Medical Education and Information Unit (ed.), Little Club Clinics in Developmental Medicine No. 12. William Heinemann Medical Books, London.

Volpe, J. J. 1975. Neurological Disorders. In: Gordon Avery (ed.), Neonatology, pp. 729–975. J. B. Lippincott Company, Philadelphia.

5 / BEHAVIORAL EVALUATION

Only in the past decade or so has the concept been established that the newborn functions at a central nervous system level higher than the merely reflexive. It is now accepted that the newborn can respond to stimulation of all five senses and can integrate his responses in a relatively sophisticated fashion. These capabilities are generally grouped under the term "behavior." Such activity may be evaluated quantitatively and qualitatively, both as a sensitive outcome measure and as a useful clinical tool. This chapter describes the latter use for newborn behavioral testing.

There are a number of general principles that should be noted as essential parts of any neonatal behavioral evaluation. One is that the examiner should measure and record the level of wakefulness or sleep in which the infant is found. This "state" (of consciousness) influences the level of response for a variety of behaviors, as well as reflex activities. For example, Moro's reflex is much more easily elicited in A-1 or S-1 than in other states. Table 5.1 describes a clinical scoring system for discrete states developed after Prechtl and Brazelton (Brazelton, 1973; Prechtl and Beintema, 1964).

Although each state is relatively discrete, the infant frequently makes smooth, almost imperceptible transitions between the awake states, and, frequently, between awake and sleep states as well. The ability to smoothly make such facile transitions on a regular basis, i.e., state cycling, is one hallmark of the normal newborn.

There is sound correlation between bioelectrical phenomena and certain sleep states. For example, state S-1 correlates with rapid eye movement sleep and its associated electroencephalographic pattern.

Another general concept is that the human newborn with an intact nervous system should be able to alter his response to repetitive stimuli. Such a capacity is described as the phenomenon of response decrement, or habituation. With presentation of a novel, simple, sensory stimulus, the response evoked diminishes with repeated applications of that same stimulus. If another, slightly different stimulus is presented, the original response will reappear. Such alteration in behavior is not fatigue (Tronick and Scanlon, in press). The typical group of responses that habituate are characterized by orienting the infant toward the stimulus. These are muscle tone changes, head and trunk turning, and autonomic nervous system alterations (such as decreased heart rate and changes in respiratory pattern). Interestingly, responses evoked by noxious stimuli, such as pain, do not diminish with repetitive stimulus application. Therefore, the examiner must carefully administer stimuli to avoid discomfort.

With these general principles in mind, we will now describe a simple, rapid system for evaluating the behavior of the full-term newborn. This system was developed to determine the effects on the neonate of maternal medication given during labor and delivery (Scanlon et al., 1974). The examination embodies state observations, certain measures of reflexive activity, and qualitative responses to several stimuli, using the sensory modalities of touch, hearing, and vision, as well as vestibular function (Moro's maneuver). There are also measures of response decrement to repeated application of several of the stimuli, measures of alertness and muscle tone, plus a subjective evaluation of whether the infant is normal. State is assessed at the start of the examination and before each specific test. The testing protocol is shown in Figure 5-1 and is described in detail below.

The *pinprick response* is elicited by gentle pin pressure on the sole of the foot while the infant lies in the supine position. Remember that excessive force will result in a noxious stimulus that does not diminish.

Table 5-1.   States of consciousness

Awake States

A-1   Eyes may be open or closed, eyelids fluttering, drowsy, or semi-dozing; activity level variable, with interspersed mild startles from time to time; reactive to sensory stimuli, but delay in response often seen; state change after stimulation frequently noted.

A-2   Eyes open, considerable motor activity with thrusting movement of extremities, even a few spontaneous startles; reactive to external stimulation with increase in startles or motor activity level. Intermittent fussing does not result in a change of state.

A-3   Alert, bright look; seems to focus attention on source of stimulation such as an object to be sucked, visual or auditory stimulus; impinging stimuli may break through, but with some delay.

A-4   Characterized by intense crying that is difficult to break through with stimulation.

Sleep States

S-1   Light sleep with eyes closed, low activity with random movements and startles; responsive to internal and external stimuli, frequently with startles or their equivalent, often with a resulting change of state.

S-2   Deep sleep with no spontaneous activity except startles at regular intervals; external stimuli produce startles with some delay; suppression of startles is rapid, and state changes are less likely.

STATE:	MANEUVER:		SCORE:		
_____	1. Response to pin prick	0	1	2	3
	Habituation no. _____				
_____	2. Resistance against passive motion				
	Pull to sitting	0	1	2	3
	Arm recoil	0	1	2	3
	Truncal tone	0	1	2	3
	General body tone	0	1	2	3
_____	3. Rooting	0	1	2	3
_____	4. Sucking	0	1	2	3
_____	5. Moro response	0	1	2	3
	Threshold (# of attempts)_____				
	Extinguishment (#)_____				
_____	6. Habituation to light in				
	eyes (#)_____				
_____	7. Response to sound	0	1	2	3
	Habituation (#)_____				
_____	8. Placing	0	1	2	3
_____	9. Alertness	0	1	2	3
_____	10. General assessment	A	B	N	S
	Reasons:				

COMMENTS:

Figure 5.1.   Testing protocol for neurobehavioral assessment of the neonate.

Generally the response has two components. One is local flexion, or withdrawal of the stimulated limb. The other is a generalized response, which includes trunk and limb motion, color change, and crying. Scoring of the response is based on withdrawal. It ranges from none to weak, delayed response, to fair, although perhaps slow, response. The optimal response is a brisk, easily elicited withdrawal. The number of stimulus applications necessary to observably change the general response is recorded as the habituation number. With this, as with the other habituation measures, the examiner should remember to let the response subside before reapplying the stimulus. No more than 12 to 14 applications of the stimulus should be given before deciding that habituation has not occurred. If the examiner follows this caveat, the question of fatigue as a mechanism, rather than habituation, is avoided.

The *resistance to passive motions examination* is comprised of four sub-examinations:

The *pull to sitting maneuver* is identical to that described under gestational age testing (Chapter 2). Head flexion is scored in a range from complete passivity, to weak resistance to great resistance with a very stiff neck. Normal head control is a forward head, with little lag when the infant is in the vertical position.

For the *arm recoil* examination, the infant's passively extended forearm is suddenly released by the examiner. Here the score's range is from absent to weak recoil, then 45°. This response may be asymmetrical. The normal is marked symmetrical recoil. Occasionally, there is very strong, rapid recoil bilaterally. This may not be completely normal and may be evidence of hyper-reflexia or hypertonicity.

During the *truncal tone* maneuver, the infant is suspended horizontally with the examiner's hand under the abdomen. Again, this is basically the same as the ventral suspension measure used in gestational age assessment in Chapter 2. Scoring ranges from extreme floppiness or hypotonia, to progressively increasing attempts to extend the head or neck, to vigorous trunk straightening. The extreme is complete rigidity in this position. This latter excessive tone score may be abnormal. The normal, unaffected newborn should maintain head and sacrum in the same plane for 3 to 5 seconds at least.

The *general body tone* examination is a subjective evaluation of the infant's muscle tone during the course of the truncal tone maneuver. Composite scoring ranges from hypotonia, to clearly weak tone, to the normal strong tone, and finally, to hypertonicity.

The *rooting reflex* scores head turning toward stimulation. A finger is touched to the corner of the infant's mouth. The baby is observed both for head turning and lip movement while supine with his head in the midline. Again, scoring ranges from no response to increasingly vigorous head turning and sucking movements.

To measure *sucking response*, the infant lies in the supine position. The proximal joint of the examiner's index finger is inserted into the infant's mouth. Scoring ranges from no or weak response, to 1 to 3 sucks per group. Long periods of vigorous sucking are normal.

Moro's maneuver is a short (10-cm) rapid, head drop when the infant is held in the supine position. The reflex response is a rapid extension of the arms, then slower flexion. Maximal response usually includes complete encirclement. Threshold is the number of head drops necessary to obtain even a minimal response. As anticipated, threshold is a crude measure of the infant's neurological responsivity. The normal infant should have some activity by the first or second application. The Moro is scaled from absent to the normal, complete, rapid response. Head drop is repeated after each response has finished to determine when the maximum response has altered. Again, no more than 12 stimulus applications (head drops) should be performed after threshold to decide on the presence of decrement.

To determine the *habituation to light*, a pen light is shone into the infant's eyes. The local response consists of eyelid closure. Once the maximal response is obtained, applications of light are done repetitively until the response obviously alters.

For *response to sound*, a bell is rung sharply within a few inches of the infant's ear while the infant is supine. The bell must be held in the midline out of sight behind the baby's head. The examiner should remember not to jostle the bassinette. Response is based on observable attentivenesss to the sound. It is scaled from no reaction or poor atten-tion, to slight change in attention level with some head turning, to search-ing or other alerting behavior to the normal of definite searching with almost immediate response to sound. Again, the stimulus is repeated at the end of each response to a maximum number of 12. When the maximal response has notably altered, the *habituation number to sound* is recorded.

For the *placing reflex*, the infant is held upright, suspended by the examiner's hands under both his axillae. The baby is slowly raised until the dorsum of his foot touches a protruding edge, usually the bassinette. Scoring is based on the ability of the stimulated leg to replace the ipsi-lateral foot back on the edge after hip and knee flexion. Scores range from no response to an easily, rapidly elicited normal response, which consists of rapid flexion of the stimulated leg, then slow extension, with eventual placing of the foot on the edge.

Alertness takes into account such difficult-to-measure variables as head turning toward a variety of environmentally encountered stimuli during the exam, widening of the eyes, brightness of the infant's face, and the infant's ability to shut out interfering stimuli. Such activity ranges from very dull responses to most stimuli, to fairly long attentive periods. Clearly, the more alert the infant, the better the score.

It should be noted that an obligatory response to the original stim-ulus, and every (unvarying) repetition without any shut-off, is not usual and may indicate abnormality. The neonate, if normal, has the ability to "filter" meaningless stimuli, especially with repeated presentations. This is the essence of habituation.

To determine the *general assessment*, the examiner is asked to appraise the infant's performance on the entire examination. This requires a value judgment and enables the examiner to synthesize the events just perceived in his own mind.

Comments allow the examiner to note unexpected occurrences and/or interfering events during the examination.

There are other, much more extensive clinical behavioral scoring systems that can be used. One of the most useful is that developed by Brazelton (Brazelton, 1973). Much of the behavioral evaluation described above was patterned after the Brazelton Scale. His system taps, in a semi-quantitative fashion, a number of integrated behavioral attributes of the newborn. The 27 subtests of the Brazelton Scale score the infant's capacity for controlling his state of consciousness, social interactional activity, physiological response to normal perinatal stress, and reflexive activity. The clinical utility of Dr. Brazelton's scale has recently been described (Soule et al., 1974); however, while extraordinarily useful for high-risk infant outcome determination, or in specific behavioral research projects, this scale is cumbersome for routine use in the typical newborn physical examination.

It should be pointed out that observations of the infant with his mother or the nursery caregiver provide an excellent opportunity to observe how the infant integrates a variety of sensory stimuli into appropriate activity. For example, a typical feeding pattern consists of the infant fussing and crying until he is picked up. Then, as the infant is moved toward breast or bottle and the nipple is offered, the infant scans the mother's (caregiver's) face. Upon recognition, there are changes in respiratory pattern, heart rate, and muscle tone as the infant nestles into the feeder's arms. Facial, head, and neck reflex activity turn the infant in the direction of the nipple, and coordinated, nutritive suckling starts. Feeding is maintained if gustatory and olfactory sensations are appropriate and the baby is not satiated. Once the latter is accomplished, the baby characteristically drifts into a deep (S-2) sleep, with concommitant alterations in autonomic activity as well as in his general response level and in his muscle tone.

In addition to these observations, the mother-infant reciprocity may also be assessed by observing other caregiving activities. The amount of time the mother holds the infant (especially face to face), how and when she talks to her new baby, even her handling (gentle, unsure, cavalier, etc.) provide the observant examiner with useful information. Such observations are an invaluable part of the neonatal physical examination.

LITERATURE CITED

Brazelton, T. B. 1973. Neonatal behavioral assessment scale. In: Clinics in Developmental Medicine, No. 50. William Heineman Medical Books, London.

Prechtl, H., and D. Beintema. 1964. The neurological examination of the full-term newborn infant. In: Clinics in Developmental Medicine, No. 12. William Heineman Medical Books, London.

Scanlon, J. W., W. U. Brown, J. B. Weiss, and M. H. Alper. 1974. Neurobehavioral responses of newborns after maternal epidural anesthesia. Anesthesiology 40:121.

Soule, A. B., K. Stanley, S. Kopans, and N. Davis. 1974. Clinical use of the Brazelton neonatal scale. Pediatrics 54:583.

Tronick, E., and J. W. Scanlon. 1978. Habituation to a localized somatosensory stimulus in the human neonate. Infant Behavior and Development. (In press).

6 / EXAMINATION OF THE SKIN, HAIR, AND NAILS

SKIN

The skin and its appendages constitute the most obvious organ system to be systematically inspected during the newborn physical examination. The skin changes dramatically in color, consistency, and transparency as the fetus matures. It may be altered by most of the serious disorders that afflict the newborn; consequently, such an accessible and responsive system deserves close attention as the examiner assesses the well-being of the newborn.

The skin consists of an epidermis (or corium) overlying the dermis (or proliferative) layer. This in turn is supported by a bed of subcutaneous tissue that is richly vascularized and, in the mature infant, contains abundant fat cells. The color of the skin is in part racially determined, but because of this rich, subcutaneous vascular network, hemoglobin contributes substantially to this attribute.

In the absence of detectable subcutaneous fatty tissue, the examiner may safely assume that there is little adipose reserve elsewhere in the body. The clinical observation is loose, hanging skin folds; the baby seems to be wearing a size 12 skin on a size 8 body. Excess extracellular fluid accumulation is easily detected in the skin and alerts one to generalized disorders of fluid and electrolyte metabolism. Pitting edema is the physical finding here, especially in dependent areas. Remember, the generally supine neonate's dependent areas are buttocks, back, and occiput.

In examining the skin, the state of the infant's behavior is irrelevant, therefore skin assessment may be left for one of the last parts of the examination. The baby should be completely unclothed so that all of the skin may be seen, and he should be warm, both for the sake of his health, and so that observed vascular phenomena may be properly interpreted.

There should be a quick overall appraisal that allows the examiner to assess general color, skin opacity, hair distribution, staining of skin, and epidermal consistency (smooth or parchment-like). The consistency of the underlying dermis is determined by palpation. A skin fold should be lifted between thumb and forefinger to obtain some estimate of the degree of development of the underlying fatty tissue.

Close attention is paid to any discontinuities in the skin's surface, or to locally demarcated pigmented or hypopigmented areas. Irregularities should be carefully described in terms of their color, tactile consistency, distribution, and depth.

The following glossary should allow accurate description of the findings.

Macule	A pigmented area less than 1 cm in diameter.
Papule	A palpably elevated area of skin less than 1 cm in diameter.
Vesicle	A blister less than 1 cm in diameter.
Pustule	A small, pus-containing vesicle.
Bulla	A larger blister of 1 cm or more in diameter.
Petechiae	Pinpoint subepidermal hemorrhages. These do not blanche with pressure.
Ecchymosis	A large area of subepidermal hemorrhage.
Erythema	A reddened area that blanches with pressure.
Induration	A loss of the usual softness of the dermis or its underlying subcutaneous tissue.
Mottling	A transient lacey pattern of dilated venous blood vessels underlying the skin.

The full-term infant is covered by a greasy, waxy white to yellowish material called *vernix caseosa*. Vernix appears early in the third trimester. It extensively covers the full-term infant but begins to diminish after 40 weeks. Post-term infants have little vernix remaining.

The skin is soft, smooth, and opaque in the full-term infant. Slight desquamation is normal over palms, soles, and in the groin. The less mature the infant, and the closer he is to birth, the more transparent is his skin. Conversely, the post-mature infant has very opaque skin, often of parchment-like quality, with desquamation of large sheets.

A fine, soft downy type of hair, called lanugo, first appears at approximately 20 weeks' gestation. It covers the body extensively, including the face. By term gestation, much of this hair has receded.

The creases of the skin, the fingernails, and the umbilical cord should be inspected for the green staining of meconium. This finding usually indicates that meconium was passed some time before birth and suggests that there may have been some transitory period of anoxia (Chapter 3).

The healthy full-term infant will have an underlying pink color especially apparent in the lips and fingernail beds. Some common variants in skin coloration are listed and described below.

1. *Pink* is the normal color of the healthy infant.
2. *Pink lips, blue hands and feet,* is acrocyanosis. It is commonly seen in the newborn less than three days of age and is of little pathological significance.
3. *Diffuse red* is seen in infants with generalized cutaneous dilation. It is common in infants less than 12 hours old but unusual thereafter.
4. *Pale* may be the color due to either decreased circulating hemoglobin or intense cutaneous vasoconstriction. In any case, it is an alarming finding and requires prompt investigation.
5. Plethora is a *ruddy, purplish* hue that suggests increased amounts of circulating hemoglobin, some of which is always unsaturated. Frequently, plethora indicates an unusually elevated hemoglobin level.
6. Cyanosis is a generalized *blue* color most intense in lips, nailbeds, and tongue, and indicates a substantial amount (more than 3 gm/dl) of unsaturated hemoglobin. Such a finding warrants prompt diagnostic attention (see Chapter 11).
7. *Yellow* indicates elevated blood concentrations of unconjugated bilirubin, which give the skin a lemon-to-orange appearance. The color is first detected on the face (where the skin overlies cartilage) and in the mucous membranes of the mouth. As the concentration of bilirubin rises, the yellow color becomes more intense, and extends further and further inferiorly, eventually staining the soles of the feet when the concentration exceeds 18 mg/dl. The "rule of threes" is sometimes helpful in estimating the bilirubin concentration during the onset of jaundice. This is:

   > Head only = 3 mg/dl
   > Head plus upper trunk = 6 mg/dl
   > Head and entire trunk = 9 mg/dl
   > Head, trunk, and upper abdomen to umbilicus = 12 mg/dl
   > Head, trunk, and entire abdomen = 15 mg/dl or greater.

8. *Greenish yellow* color is imparted to the skin by elevated blood concentrations of conjugated bilirubin, usually in the range of 3 to 5 mg/dl.
9. *Slate grey* color is due to significant amounts of methemoglobin. Infants in profound peripheral vascular collapse and cyanosis may also appear grey.

Diffuse hyperpigmentation (from melanocytes) is unusual, but may be seen in some infants with adrenal insufficiency, as well as with certain other metabolic disorders.

Some of the common dermal findings in newborns are transitory and some are permanent. The more evanescent lesions are described first.

1. *Petechiae* appear as discrete blue-black pinpoint macules. They gradually change and fade by the third to fourth day. They cannot be obviously blanched by pressure. This is a distinctive hallmark. If sparsely scattered petechiae appear at birth, and then disappear, they were probably related to the normal trauma of delivery.

    Scattered petechiae should be differentiated from profuse petechiae, which appear in recurrent crops suggesting some ongoing process, often systemic (and usually serious) in nature.

2. *Ecchymoses* are large areas of subcutaneous hemorrhage. They are generally more localized than petechiae, but have the same type of natural course. Ecchymoses are not generally seen in full-term infants, but may be seen over the presenting part in breech or traumatic deliveries.

3. *Reddened circular marks* over the face, especially anterior to the ears, are suggestive of minor trauma from forceps application. Occasionally, these areas develop underlying induration of fat necrosis, and rarely, the underlying necrotic tissue may drain. When these marks are seen, the examiner should remember to check carefully for facial nerve paralysis as described in Chapter 4.

4. *Abrasions and lacerations* occasionally occur during delivery. They should be noted and accurately recorded.

5. Other common transitory lesions not trauma-related include milia, miliaria, pustular melanosis, and erythema toxicum.

    Milia may be present at birth and are localized to the nose, forehead, and cheeks. Milia are discrete, pinhead-sized white papules of keratogenous material that disappear within the first several weeks of life.

    Miliaria may develop within the first 12 hours after birth and is the result of obstructed eccrine sweat ducts; thus, its distribution is that of the sweat glands. The usual sites for this pinpoint vesiculopapular disorder are the forehead, scalp, and skin folds. If the obstruction is superficial, the lesions appear as thin-walled grouped vesicles (miliaria crystalina). If the obstruction is deep, the lesions appear as grouped red papules (miliaria rubra). Miliaria may clear within the first few days to 1 week if the infant is not over-heated.

The lesions of *pustular melanosis* may be confused with miliaria. At an early stage in their evolution they appear as small (2-mm) vesicopustules with a distributional predilection for the forehead, neck, and submental area. They may occur in any other area of the body, including palms and soles. The intact vesicle finally ruptures to reveal a pigmented macule surrounded by a fine, scaly skin ring. In contrast to miliaria, these lesions may be present at birth. Stains of the vesicopustule's contents reveal amorphous debris and polymorphonuclear leukocytes, but no organisms. Pustular melanosis is more frequent in the black neonate.

Erythema toxicum is, by far, the most variable, as well as the most common, of the benign transient lesions of the newborn. It consists of irregular erythematous macules or patches involving virtually any area of the body except the palms and soles. The lesions usually appear around the second day, but new ones may appear over the first week or more. The erythematous macules usually contain a central papule, which may be yellow or white, depending on the infant's serum bilirubin level. The lesions, especially the macular type, may vanish rapidly. The eruption generally persists for only a few days, and occurs more often in full-term infants than in less mature babies. These pustules contain eosinophils and are sterile.

These benign lesions must be differentiated from the macular, vesicular, or pustular eruptions associated with infectious diseases. Close attention to the antecedent history, the infant's general health, the presence or absence of adenopathy, and the results of Gram's or Giemsa's stain from suspicious lesions should allow the examiner to distinguish between innocent and more ominous lesions.

Hemangiomas are common developmental vascular anomalies in the newborn. The full classification of these anomalies is beyond the scope of this chapter, and the reader is referred to an excellent review of vascular malformations by Margileth (Margileth, 1976) for further discussion. However, common variants are briefly described here.

Flat macular hemangiomas are quite common, and are usually found over the nape of the neck, the eyelids, and the glabella. These hemangiomas have indistinct borders and are a salmon-pink color. They are easily blanched to the color of the underlying skin. They usually disappear by one year of age.

The nevus flammeus, or port-wine stain, is much less common. It is sharply delineated and blanches only slightly with pressure. Its color is purple to red in light-skinned babies but appears jet black in black newborns. These hemangiomata do not involute, and if distributed over the trigeminal territory of the face, may be accompanied by an angiomatous malformation of the brain.

Raised hemangiomatous lesions are less commonly found. The strawberry hemangioma is a bright red vascular tumor with sharply demarcated margins. It is somewhat compressible, and blanches with pressure to reveal some underlying pigmentation. Deeper cavernous hemagiomata may have their margins obscured by the overlying epidermal tissue, but usually impart a reddish blue color to the overlying tissue. These tumors are also somewhat compressible. They tend to increase in size, occasionally very rapidly, after birth.

A number of pigmented lesions are common in the newborn. Of these, the most frequent is the Mongolian spot. This is a large, gray-blue pigmented area seen in the lumbosacral area at birth in the majority of black, oriental, and American Indian infants (and rarely in Caucasians). The pigmented area is of no clinical significance (although often alarming to mothers) and usually disappears during the first few years of life.

Café-au-lait spots are brown macules or patches, usually less than 3 cm in diameter. They are occasionally seen in the newborn period, but occur at some time in 20% of normal children. Small café-au-lait spots are not significant, but children with larger than usual spots (4–6 cm in area), or who have more than 6 spots may develop an underlying neurofibromatosis.

Junctional nevi are flat, pigmented lesions, ranging from brown to black in color. They are usually less than 1 cm in diameter. Junctional nevi are seen in up to 15% of black infants and are usually without significance. If large numbers of these nevi are apparent at birth, such syndromes as tuberous sclerosis, xeroderma pigmentosus, and generalized neurofibromatosis should be considered.

Eczema is a reactive response of the skin to some systemic allergen or primary local irritant. The end response is quite similar in both situations. The skin first reddens, then begins to break down with micro-vesicles. The lesion oozes fluid, finally dries, and then scaling of the overlying injured skin occurs. The most common distribution involves the diaper area. If the skin stays wet it may become macerated and infected. In some infants the scaling lesions have a greasy feeling. This is termed seborrheic eczema, and usually involves the scalp, where it is commonly labeled "cradle cap."

Some infants have an eczematoid-appearing rash in the diaper region that, on closer inspection shows small (0.5 cm to 1 cm), superficial satellite lesions, peripheral to the reddened area. These satellite lesions suggest an infection by *Candida albicans* (*moniliasis*). This diagnosis is proven by appropriate cultures.

Most of the common lesions of the newborn skin have been described. The number of aberrations that may occur in the newborn skin is enormous. The reader is referred to appropriate sources for help in distinguishing among these less common conditions (Esterly and Solomon, 1973; Margileth, 1976; Solomon and Esterly, 1973).

HAIR

The hair is rarely involved as an isolated finding. The quality of newborn hair is usually quite different from adult hair consistency. However, it must be noted that a number of syndromes exist that, in part, are characterized by the pattern of hair distribution. If the infant appears to have an unusual quantity or distribution of hair, or brittle or abnormally textured hair, texts such as D. W. Smith's classic monograph (Smith, 1970) dealing with recognizable patterns of human malformation should be consulted.

NAILS

The nails of the full-term infant usually extend byond the nail bed. The nails may be involved in a number of syndromes, the most frequent aberrations involving some element of hypoplasia. Spoon-shaped, dysplastic, or absent nails are manifestations of such systemic disorders as the fetal alcohol and anti-convulsant syndromes. Absent or aberrant nails may be associated with absent patellae, plus renal and iliac bone anomalies in a rare syndrome of osteo-onychia dysplasia. This latter relationship is a gratuitous pearl from the authors, and ends this chapter.

LITERATURE CITED

Esterly, N. B., and L. M. Solomon. 1973. Diseases of the skin. In: R. E Behrman (ed.), Neonatal-Perinatal Medicine, pp. 905–936. C. V. Mosby Company, St. Louis.

Margileth, A. M. 1976. Dermatologic conditions. In: G. B. Avery (ed.), Neonatology, pp. 899–943. J. B. Lippincott Company, Philadelphia.

Smith, D. W. 1970. Recognizable Syndromes of Congenital Malformation. W. B. Saunders Company, Philadelphia.

Solomon, L. M., and N. B. Esterly. 1973. Neonatal Dermatology. W. B. Saunders Company, Philadelphia.

7 / EXAMINATION OF THE SKELETAL SYSTEM

GENERAL

The newborn's skeletal system is examined by inspection, palpation, and, on occasion, by listening. The components of this system are the bones, their supporting and connecting tissues, and the joints. The examiner will be noting movement, shape, and size relationships during the inspection. When indicated by history or physical exam, special maneuvers are occasionally required. The reader is referred to several general sources for further clinical details (Griffin, 1976; Lloyd-Roberts, 1971; Smith, 1977).

The size and shape relationships between the different parts of the infant's body should be assessed in the initial inspection of the skeletal support system. General symmetry between the two sides of the body is expected. Measurements of thoracic length and extremities are recorded if observation suggests a discrepancy. Normal values for these measurements and their relationships depend on gestational age. Congenital abnormalities of the skeletal system can be diagnosed by determining the ratio of the length of the body above the waist, to the length below the waist, which should not exceed 1.7 in the full-term newborn. A higher ratio implies congenitally shortened lower extremities, as in archrondroplasia.

General inspection also provides information on posture and spontaneous movement. During the initial physical exam, the posture of the baby usually reflects the position of the fetus in utero. Orthopaedic abnormality is suspected when an unusual posture cannot be changed by passive joint manipulation. A repeat skeletal exam during the first week of life is needed to assess the change over time from the initially observed posture. In this regard, a history of the postconceptual age and type of delivery is helpful. For example, breech-delivered infants frequently lie with their hips abducted and knees flexed. Range of joint motion and posture vary with maturity and type of presentation at delivery. Fractures should be suspected from a history of difficult delivery or a report of a "snapping" noise during birth. Painful, limited movement of the broken extremity is characteristic. Palpation often elicits crying.

SPINE

The curvature of the spine is observed and palpated. Recognizable abnormalities include scoliosis, lordosis, or kyphosis. Lateral curvature found on the initial exam is usually due to in-utero positioning. A follow-up exam is necessary to show resolution of asymmetry. Passive flexion, extension, and lateral bending of the spine are then performed. The presence of masses or openings in the overlying skin are specifically noted. Masses in the spinal area may be meningomyeloceles and can be covered by skin, subcutaneous tissue, or meninges. The examination of any mass in this area should be done in a completely sterile fashion because openings in the skin overlying the spine represent communication with the spinal canal. Abnormalities of the vertebrae are often not identifiable through physical exam and require radiological evaluation. A history or physical finding of decreased anal sphincter tone, abnormal bladder function, or neurological abnormality in the lower extremity should lead the examiner to suspect a spinal cord defect.

UPPER EXTREMITY

Skeletal examination of the upper extremity includes clavicle, scapula, and proximal humerus, followed by evaluation of the arm, elbow, forearm, and hand. Normal values for range of motion in the joints and body units of the upper extremity are listed in Table 7-1.

The clavicles are inspected and palpated over their entire length for size, contour, masses, or crepitance. A fractured clavicle may be suspected when there is a history of difficult delivery, particularly a breech birth. Irregularity or crepitance on palpation, and decreased movement of the shoulder, are signs of a fractured clavicle. The scapulae are inspected and palpated while the infant is resting. Contour, sym-

Table 7-1.   Range of motion in upper extremities

Joint or Bony Unit	Flexion	Extension	Abduction	External Rotation	Internal Rotation
Shoulder	Close to 180°	≥25°	Close to 180°	≥45°	≥80°
Elbow	145°	165–170°			
Forearm				(Supination)[a] ≥80°	(Pronation)[a] ≥80°
Wrist	75–80°	65°–75°			
Digits	Able to clench	Full extension			
Metacarpal-Phalangeal		0°			
Interphalangeal		0° → 5°–15°			

[a] These maneuvers are done while the humerus is held immobile and elbow is at 90°.

metry, and movement of the shoulder are observed. Range of joint motion itself is evaluated both by noting voluntary motion and by passive manipulation. Length and contour of the humerus are examined. It may also be fractured during a difficult delivery. The examiner may feel a mass due to hematoma formation, or elicit signs of pain from the baby during palpation.

The elbow, forearm, and wrist are examined for the number, size, and contour of the bones. The range of motion of the joints and bony units is assessed. Absence of either radius or ulna can be diagnosed on physical exam, and is often associated with other congenital defects. Flexion of the wrist is greater in the full-term baby than it is in the preterm baby.

The hand should be examined in detail, not only because a great number of congenital anomalies of the hand itself are possible, but also because manual anomalies are often part of a more generalized syndrome. The shape, size, and posture of the hand are initially examined. The average full-term infant's hand length, from the tip of his middle finger to the base of his palm, is 6.75 cm ± 1.25 cm. The ratio of middle-finger length to total hand length is normally .38 to .48 in the newborn. The digits are examined for number, shape, and length. The space between them and their range of motion are also noted. The nails are examined for their surface characteristics, such as color, pits, spooning, or hypoplasia. Absent nails should also be recorded. The palm is inspected for the arrangement of the creases. Further information may be obtained by performing specialized dermatoglyphic analysis of whorls, ridges, and loops on the fingertips, although such an analysis is not a part of the routine examination.

LOWER EXTREMITY

The lower extremities are inspected for posture, symmetry, size, contour, and range of motion. Norms for range of joint motion in the lower extremities are listed in Table 7-2.

The normal posture of the full-term newborn delivered by cephalic presentation is hip and knee flexion. Breech delivery may cause more flexion of the hips and extension of the knees, so that the baby may appear to be attempting to put his foot in his mouth. These findings have usually disappeared by the subsequent examination (if not, congenital hip dislocation should be suspected). The upper legs are palpated for the presence of crepitance or masses. Fractures of the femur, tibia, or fibula can take place at birth, causing irregularity or mass due to hematoma formation. Femoral fractures may have massive but occult blood loss

Table 7-2.   Range of motion in lower extremities

Joint or Extremity	Flexion	Extension	Abduction	Adduction	Internal Rotation	External Rotation
Hip	145°		90°	10°–20°	40°	80°
Knee	120°–145°	90°				
Ankle	*Dorsiflexion* Above resting position *Plantar Flexion* > 10° from resting position					
Forefoot			≥ 10°–15°	≥ 10°–15°		
Hindfoot			valgus ≥ 10°	varus ≥ 5°		

into the surrounding soft tissues and muscles. To look for discrepancies in femoral length, both knees are flexed beyond the right angle while the feet are apposed and the tips of the big toes are in the same horizontal plane. The examiner faces the feet, and notes the level of the highest point of both knees.

The hips are put through their full range of motion and the integrity of the hip joint is evaluated. The hips of the newborn normally have some flexion contracture, which gradually decreases during the first three months of life. An important diagnostic possibility that must be evaluated in every neonate is *congenital hip dysplasia* (CHD). Several tests are routinely used, one of these being Ortolani's maneuver, which is performed by the examiner placing his fingers on the trochanters bilaterally while the thumbs grip the medial aspects of the femurs. With the knees *and* the hips flexed, the thighs are first adducted, then they are fully abducted. CHD is likely if the examiner feels a jerking motion when the femoral head passes over the acetabulum. A second maneuver, Barlow's test, requires the examiner to place pressure with his thumb backward over the head of the femur with the hip and knee flexed to 90°. An audible, palpable, and, occasionally, visible "clunk" denotes instability of the hip, permitting backward dislocation of the femoral head. Pressure in the reverse direction with the examiner's fingers placed behind the greater trochanter produces a similar "clunk" of reduction. Creases in the buttocks are inspected and, if asymmetrical, should arouse further suspicions of hip abnormality. If abnormalities are noted, a radiological evaluation and an orthopaedic consultation are required.

The knees are inspected for their contour and range of motion and for the presence and location of the patella. With decreasing gestational maturity, the ability for extension approaches 180°.

The lower legs are examined primarily for length and shape. Internal rotation of the lower legs and the presence of bowing (without signficant shortening) are normal in the newborn, except when bowing is in an *anterior* direction. This latter circumstance indicates the presence of sclerotic or dyplastic bone. Such a finding requires orthopaedic attention and further study. Palpation should confirm the presence of the tibia and fibula, and note any irregularities in contour. When the tibia is absent, the foot is in a varus position; when the fibula is absent, the foot is in a valgus position.

The ankles and feet are observed while the infant is at rest, then while in spontaneous activity and after stimulation. Passive motion of the ankle in both dorsiflexion and plantar flexion is initially dependent on prenatal positioning. Dorsiflexion of the ankle is more limited in the preterm infant than it is in the full-term baby. The digits of the foot are counted, then their size and the spaces between them are observed. The sole is inspected; its creases are useful in the estimation of gestational maturity (Chapter 2).

The range of motion of both the fore- and hindfoot are evaluated. If there is equinovarus with adduction of the forefoot at rest, the examiner may try to overcome it by attempting to abduct the forefoot and touch the little toe to the outside of the leg, without using undue force. If this maneuver is successful, then the varus deformity is probably functional and not pathological.

The examiner should remember that even minimal deformities, while unimportant to him and inconsequential to the infant, may elicit great anxiety in the parents; therefore, he must be patient and reassuring in his explanation.

LITERATURE CITED

Griffin, P. D. 1976. Orthopaedics in the Newborn. In: Gordon Avery (ed.), Neonatology. J. B. Lippincott Company, Philadelphia.

Lloyd-Roberts, G. C. 1971. Orthopaedic Abnormalities. In: A. P. Normal (ed.), Congenital Abnormalities in Infancy. Blackwell Scientific Publications, London.

Smith, D. W. 1977. Recognizable Patterns of Human Malformation. 2nd Ed. W. B. Saunders Company, Philadelphia.

8 / EXAMINATION OF THE HEAD, EARS, NOSE, MOUTH, AND NECK

THE HEAD

The head of the newborn delivered spontaneously and vaginally from a vertex position is usually irregular in shape because of molding. Overriding of the sutures is common, and, frequently, there is subcutaneous edema over the presenting part. This is called *caput succedaneum*, and should be differentiated from the relatively less common cephalohematoma, which is a subgalleal collection of blood. As such, it is bounded by the suture lines. Unlike the "caput," which is most pronounced at birth and subsides within 2–3 days, the cephalohematoma increases in size up to 3 days, and is usually not obvious at the time of delivery. The center often liquifies after 3–4 days, giving the feel of fluctuance. Although most resolve completely, infrequently a pea-sized, calcified knot may remain for months. Outer-table skull fractures have been found in about 20% of cephalohematomas.

A well-rounded head is characteristic of infants delivered by cesarean section without antecedent labor. Those delivered by breech presentation may be molded in a more posterior direction, giving the head an egg-shaped configuration.

There are three types of defective closure of the cranial end of the neural tube that are evident immediately at birth. These are:

Anencephaly, which is the absence of both the membranous skull and the cerebral hemispheres;

Encephalocele, which is a herniation of the brain and meninges through a defect in the skull, resulting in a sac-like structure (75% occur in the occipital area—these have a poor prognosis); and

Cranial meningocele, which is a bony defect that contains only meninges (it is associated with a fairly good prognosis).

After observation, the examiner should carefully palpate the skull bones, sutures, and fontanels. The main sutures to be noted during the routine examination are:

the *coronal*, which separates the frontal from the parietal bones;

the *sagittal*, which runs longitudinally in the midline between the two
parietal bones;

the *lambdoidal*, which extends posterolaterally from the posterior
fontanel and separates the occipital from the parietal bones; and

the *squamous*, which separates parietal from temporal bones. Since the
intramembranous temporal bone abuts the enchondreal cancellous
bone of the skull's base, this suture widens early when intracranial
pressure increases.

In the first few days of life, many infants have overlapping of the
cranial bones because of molding, and ridges that may be felt instead of
patent sutures. When in doubt, the examiner should reinvestigate the
sutures in a few days.

At birth, as many as six fontanels can be palpated (Figure 8-1),
although the anterior and posterior fontanels are by far the most
important. The anterior fontanel (AF) is easily palpated as a diamond-
shaped soft area at the junction of the coronal and sagittal sutures. It
usually measures 5×4 cm at its widest points. The triangular posterior
fontanel, between the sagittal and lambdoidal sutures, is smaller, but also
often patent at birth.

The anterior fontanel normally closes during the first 18 months of
life. The posterior fontanel closes during the last two months before
birth, or in the first two months following birth. Increased intracranial
pressure may first be manifest by fullness or bulging of the anterior
fontanel. Occasionally, arterial pulsations can be observed in the normal
fontanel, but when seen may suggest either an over-full anterior fontanel,
or increased arterial pressure. A sunken fontanel is a late finding in cases
of severe dehydration.

Premature closure of one or more of the cranial sutures is a
pathological condition known as *craniosynostosis*. Closure of a suture
inhibits growth of the skull perpendicular to the line of osseous fusion
and results in distortion of the head shape. Thus, craniosynostosis may
lead to a variety of head shapes depending on the number and position
of the sutures involved. Table 8-1 notes common nomenclature and
findings.

The small head with closed sutures with a *normal* shape is the result
of abnormal brain development. In these infants, closure of the sutures is
secondary to failure of brain growth.

On palpation of the skull, the examiner should be alerted to any
depression or irregularity that suggests a fracture. These must be
followed up with the appropriate x-rays. Soft areas of bone (craniotabes)

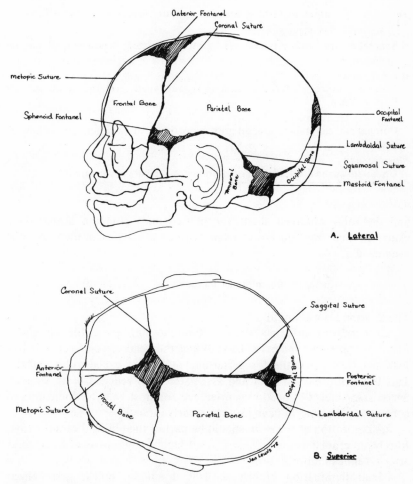

Figure 8-1. Two views of the neonatal skull showing clinically important fontanels and sutures.

may also be present anywhere over the skull, but are most common in the parietal areas. They are usually of no clinical significance.

Measurement of the head circumference is an essential part of the newborn examination. A paper tape measure (non-stretching) is placed around the head at the widest point, and a reading taken and recorded. If much molding has occurred, the value can be falsely low. The measurement must be repeated within the first week, and again, definitely, prior to the infant's discharge. Head circumference varies with gestational age,

Table 8-1.   Common patterns of premature suture closure (craniosynostosis)

Scaphocephaly (Dolichocephaly)
  Sagittal suture closure; lateral head growth restricted; head enlarged anterior to posterior

Brachycephaly
  Coronal suture closure; excessive lateral head growth; head appears foreshortened

Oxycephaly (Acrocephaly)
  Coronal and sagittal closure; all growth restricted, often resulting in a "tower" shaped head

Plagiocephaly
  Unilateral coronal suture closure; asymmetrical head growth laterally

---

and the value obtained should be plotted on a standard head-growth chart. In this way, deviation from normal can be quantified. As one general rule:

$$\text{the head circumference (cm)} = \frac{\text{length (cm)}}{2} + 10$$

This is accurate usually to ±1.5 cm.

A head circumference greater than the 90th percentile for gestational age is called macrocephaly. When the head circumference is less than the 10th percentile for gestational age, it is called microcephaly. This is usually pathological and associated with reduced brain volume. Serial assessments of head circumference are most valuable indicators of normal or pathological head growth in early infancy.

Auscultation of the skull should be part of the physical examination. Rarely, a cranial bruit is heard; it is highly suggestive of a cerebral arterio-venous malformation.

Transillumination of the skull is a simple, quick, and helpful maneuver in the assessment of an abnormally large or unusually shaped head, or when neurological appraisal suggests brain abnormality. In the absence of prominent, superficial scalp edema, transillumination is increased with:

1. abnormal collections of fluid within the cranial vault;
2. the presence of an extremely thin cerebral mantle (usually associated with hydrocephalus); and
3. extreme thinning of the cranial bones, seen in certain congenital chondro or osteo dystrophies.

Remember, also, that thick hair or deeply pigmented skin will influence transillumination. Any asymmetrical transillumination must be evaluated

further. It should be noted that transillumination is only an aid to diagnosis, and must be used in conjunction with a more specific and detailed
investigation before a definite diagnosis can be established.

THE EAR

An irregular shape of the ear, asymmetry, or extremes in its size or position on the head should suggest to the examiner that there may be
associated congenital anomalies. It is beyond the scope of this book to
describe the full range of congenital morphological abnormalities that
are associated with abnormal ears. The reader is referred to the text by
Smith (Smith, 1970) for a more complete discussion.

Abnormalities, such as auricular or pre-auricular pits, or fleshy
appendages, such as lipomas or skin tags, may also be part of a syndro-
matic constellation. Again, the reader is referred to standard textbooks
on recognizable congenital syndromes for more detail.

Visualization of the canal and eardrum of the newborn is difficult,
but should be performed if indicated by history or other findings. A
2-mm otoscope head should be used. The infant should be firmly immo-
bilized, with his ear canal pointing directly at the ceiling. One of the
examiner's hands is used for cephalic immobilization while the other
hand grasps the otoscope.

The pinna should be tugged down and backward in order to
straighten the canal for adequate viewing of the tympanic membrane.
Careful, slow advancement of the otoscope is necessary because of the
very short distances encountered.

The more superior and horizontal orientation of the tympanic
membrane in the neonate changes the relationship between short and
long processes of the maleus. The small size of the newborn's canal in
relation to the otoscope head necessitates, through manipulation of the
pinna, a piecemeal examination of the drum to thoroughly visualize all
quadrants of the membrane. The normal drum is less lustrous in the
newborn than in an older child. Its vascularity is also increased, particularly immediately after birth. Occasionally, if the infant cries, a rapidly
appearing, then disappearing, red blush is seen. This is quite normal.

Although rare, bulging of the membrane because of fluid in the middle ear will sometimes be seen. A red color indicates acute otitis media.
A blue or black color indicates hemmorhage, which usually implies
trauma or, less frequently, a bleeding diathesis. An amber or clear color
suggests non-suppurative, serous fluid.

The use of the pneumatic otoscope is not routine for the newborn
examination: Excessive pressure changes may collapse the thin walls of

the baby's auditory canal and result in trauma. The information obtained is usually less than the risk involved. Clearly, questions of serious ear abnormality should be promptly referred to an otorhinolaryngologist.

Hearing

Based on extensive clinical and laboratory studies there is no doubt that the human newborn can "hear," and has a very sophisticated ability to appreciate nuances in sound. However, the clinical appraisal of hearing during the routine newborn examination is still very limited. A typical method is to observe the infant's response to loud noises, such as a hand clap or a loud shout. The infant will often stiffen, startle, and/or cry. Even if care if taken not to introduce other stimuli at the same time, this technique is still very crude.

The examiner is advised to use some of the techniques described in Chapter 5 to attempt a simplified answer to the question "Can this baby hear?" First of all the infant's response to a gently ringing bell or a softly shaken rattle can be observed using the criteria described under the neurobehavioral examination (Chapter 5). Several repeated examinations may reassure the examiner of response and thus the gross normality of the auditory apparatus. Another maneuver is to assess the baby's response to a spoken voice when the infant is held in the midline facing the examiner. With this technique, another person speaks softly to the infant from either side and the response is observed. Head turning toward the voice is the most frequently seen response. The ability of the newborn to lateralize sound and to preferentially respond to a female voice has been demonstrated. Such neonatal capacity can be observed during the routine physical examination using the above maneuver.

Asking the mother herself whether she has any question concerning the infant's ability to hear often proves useful. Mothers are extremely perceptive (perhaps overly sensitive) observers of their infant's ability. If a mother indicates that her baby doesn't seem to respond to her voice, further otologic and auditory investigation is warranted. Hearing evaluation can be carried out in the newborn period using new techniques of evoked brainstem responses and computer averaging of the resultant evoked potentials (Starr et al., 1977). This investigative technique holds enormous promise for the future of newborn hearing testing.

THE NECK

Examination of the newborn's neck consists of inspection, palpation, and auscultation. Transillumination should be used if there are abnormal masses present.

The infant's neck is relatively short, especially in chubby infants, in whom this shortness is accentuated. Redundant skin at the posterolateral part is called "web neck" and is commonly found in Turner's and Noonan's syndromes (Smith, 1970).

The neck should be palpated posteriorly along the cervical spine, laterally over the sternomastoid and trapezius muscles, and anteriorly to define the larynx, cricoid area, and thyroid gland. While examining the neck, each clavicle should be palpated for possible fractures. A history of difficult or breech delivery should increase the diligence of this search.

Occasionally, the newborn infant is noted to have torticollis. This is a spasmodic, unilateral contraction of the neck muscles resulting in the head tilting toward the deranged muscle and the chin tipping away from that side. In most instances, this is caused by a traumatic hematoma of the sternomastoid muscle, acquired either in utero or during delivery. It usually resolves without specific treatment. Rarely, both web neck and torticollis may be found together in maldevelopment of the cervical vertebrae such as the Klippel-Feil syndrome.

The rich blood supply to the posterior neck, especially at the hair line, give rise to a visible red splotch euphemistically called "a stork bite." Mothers rarely miss it. The inexperienced examiner may mistake this for an hemangioma.

The *cystic hygroma* is the commonest mass found in the neck. It is a soft, multilocular, fluctuant swelling arising from lymph tissue and found most frequently in the posterior triangle. It transilluminates very easily in contrast to other cystic or solid masses in the neck. These denser masses are chiefly brachial cleft cysts, and arise in the anterior triangle.

Thyroid swellings are uncommon except in endemic goiter areas, and in infants whose mothers have either taken medication containing iodine or anti-thyroid drugs. Recently, goiter associated with repeated iodine skin preparation has been described (Chabrolle and Rossier, 1978). Such goiters are usually readily palpable, may occasionally be visible, and, rarely, can be large enough to cause tracheal compression.

At birth it is distinctly unusual to find palpable lymph nodes in the neck or post auricular area. Their presence should alert the examiner to the possibility of congenital infection.

THE NOSE

The nose of the normal newborn is symmetrical and relatively flat in comparison to that of the older child or adult. There is no visible movement of the nose with normal breathing. Flaring of the alae nasi is a constant sign of increased respiratory effect and needs investigation. The base of the nose can either be abnormally wide or narrow. When suspicion is aroused by observation, the distance between the two inner canthi should be measured, Widening of the base of the nose (> 2.5 cm in the term infant) and consequently widely spaced eyes is called *hypertelorism*. This results from over development of the lesser wings of the sphenoid bone. This is a common finding in many congenital syndromes, in contrast to the rarity of its counterpart, *hypotelorism*, which is found exclusively in infants with trisomy 13 or holoprosencephaly.

The space between the eyes and lower forehead is richly supplied with blood. Prominent redness may appear here and suggests hemangiomata. It is not, and the examiner should allay any maternal anxieties.

On the whole, congenital structural nasal abnormalities are uncommon. When they occur they are most often part of a more generalized syndrome. Nasal asymmetry and/or extreme flattening are infrequent, and represent either congenital hypoplasia or an acquired dislocation of the triangular cartilage. The latter diagnosis can be confirmed by returning the nasal tip to the midline and observing the protruding septum through the alae (Jazbi, 1974).

Choanal atresia is a common abnormality of the nasal passages. Since neonates breathe nasally by preference, when bilateral atresia occurs it may appear as a cyanotic infant with a severe airway obstruction. This can be effectively managed by opening the infant's mouth to establish an oral airway. Unilateral choanal atresia, on the other hand, often remains undiagnosed until later in childhood when it appears either as persistent nasal discharge from the affected side or as unequal, noisy, nasal breathing, usually during upper respiratory infections. A soft, #5, French catheter should be passed through each nostril to confirm patency in every suspected infant. It need not, however, be part of the routine exam.

The maxillary antrums and the ethmoid and sphenoidal sinuses are all present at birth, and are usually of sufficient size and aeration to harbor infection. The frontal sinus does not develop until after the second year of life and is thus an unimportant infection focus in the newborn period. Sinusitis is relatively rare early in infancy, but it must be kept in mind as a possibility in those few instances when persistent nasal discharge becomes apparent.

THE MOUTH

Examination of the mouth consists of close inspection and palpation of the lips, gums, tongue, palate, and oropharynx.

A small oral opening, or *microstomia*, occurs in a few generalized syndromes, the most frequent of which are trisomies 18 and 21 (Down syndrome). Macrostomia, on the other hand, is frequent in the mucopolysaccharidoses, but is otherwise rare. Downturning corners of the mouth, or "fish mouth," in another uncommon finding, but may be observed in the fetal alcohol syndrome.

Cleft lip and palate are obvious oral abnormalities. Cleft lip is a lateral defect that may occur alone or together with a cleft palate. It can vary from a niche in the lip (more often on the left side) to complete separation (usually bilateral) extending up into the floor of the nose. The more severe types are usually associated with a cleft palate. Cleft lip also has a high frequency of other associated oral malformations, which range from bifid uvula to complete absence of the hard palate. Infants with large defects may have associated midline brain defects and should be carefully and completely evaluated for such possibilities.

Epstein's pearls are small white accumulations of epithelial cells frequently found on either side of the median raphe of the palate, or on the gums. They are of no clinical significance and disappear spontaneously within a few weeks. Mothers invariably spot them.

The tongue of the full-term newborn appears relatively big, but true macroglossia is infrequent, although it does occur with congenital hypothyroidism, the mucopolysaccharidoses, intrinsic lingual tumors, and Beckwith's syndrome. This latter is the association of large birthweight, visceromegaly, umbilical abnormalities, intractable hypoglycemia, and macroglossia. Aglossia and hypoglossia are very rare, and are always associated with other anomalies. Deviation of the tongue to one side occurs with lower cranial nerve palsy. In this instance other signs of neurological deficit are usually also present.

There is a wide variation in the length and thickness of the normal frenulum, thus "tongue-tie" is very frequently over diagnosed and overtreated. Limitation of tongue movement severe enough to interfere with sucking or later speech development is extremely uncommon. The authors are doubtful if such ever warrants surgical intervention.

Small bluish white swellings of variable size (ranulas) are occasionally found on the floor of the mouth, and represent benign mucous gland retention cysts. They rarely require anything more than observation and maternal reassurance.

Natal teeth are seen infrequently, occurring about once in 2,000 births. They erupt chiefly at the position of the lower incisors and may either be supernumerary or prematurely erupted teeth. Most of them are precariously attached to the gingival margin, making risk of their aspiration high. As a general rule, they should be removed as soon as possible after birth.

Micrognathia, or mandibular hypoplasia, is a more frequent abnormality of the mouth. It may occur alone, but usually has other associated anomalies. The Pierre-Robin syndrome, which includes glossoptosis, pseudomacroglossia, and high-arched or cleft palate, is a common cause of micrognathia. Such peculiar looking infants are most often of normal intelligence and benefit greatly from aggressive medical care.

The oro-pharynx is an unusual site for abnormality in the newborn and thus receives little attention during the normal physical examination. Indeed, vigorous manipulation of the newborn's oro-pharynx may "reward" the examiner with significant apnea and bradycardia caused by the initation of vagal reflexes. A quick glance during the month examination should suffice to rule out tumors and serious structural abnormality in the posterior pharynx. On the other hand, a history of polyhydramnios or excessive oral secretions after birth should alert the examiner that esophageal atresia (and its frequently associated tracheo-esophageal fistula) may be present. Early recognition of this problem is crucial, because best results are obtained by early surgical intervention.

The diagnosis can be confirmed by passing a radiopaque catheter through the mouth. Passage will be stopped a variable distance below the mouth and before the stomach is reached. X-ray reveals the curled-up opaque feeding tube within the blind esophageal pouch. Please note that the introduction of contrast material is not necessary (and perhaps contraindicated) in diagnosing the lesion. If the x-ray reveals air in the stomach, the presence of a tracheo-esophageal fistula below the atresia is demonstrated. The physical finding of a dilated, air-filled stomach is an important clue in this situation.

LITERATURE CITED

Chabrolle, J. P., and A. Rossier. 1978. Goitre and hypothyroidism in the newborn after cutaneous absorption of iodine. Arch. Dis. Child. 53:495.

Jazbi, B. 1974. Nasal septum deformity in the newborn. Clin. Pediatr. 13:953.

Smith, D. W. 1970. Recognizable Patterns of Human Malformation. W. B. Saunders Company, Philadelphia.

Starr, A. R., N. Amlie, W. H. Martin, and S. Sanders. 1977. Development of auditory function in newborn infants revealed by auditory brainstem potentials. Pediatrics 60:831.

9 / EXAMINATION OF THE EYES

Examination of the newborn eye is, at times, neglected by the busy physician, or is confined to a quick examination of the conjunctiva for signs of infection. The other extreme, a full examination of the newborn eye, requires experience with the indirect ophthalmoscope and may take more than 30 minutes. Some balance must be struck between these two approaches; this is the purpose of this chapter. Clinical details and associations may be found in the references at the chapter's end (Adler, 1966; Read and Goldberg, 1977).

Because this text is directed toward the inexperienced neonatal examiner, there is no attempt made to be comprehensive in describing the findings in the newborn eye. It is assumed that all infants with significant abnormal findings, and those infants at high risk for eye disease, will be seen by an ophthalmologist. This latter group particularly includes pre-term infants who have been treated with oxygen and are therefore subject to retrolental fibroplasia.

An important point: an adequate examination of the lens and fundus requires dilation of the pupils. This is accomplished by instilling one drop each of 0.5% cyclopentolate and 2.5% phenylephrine in each eye. If pupillary dilation has not occurred within 45 minutes, a second drop of each may be instilled. This dosage should be safe in the full-term newborn, but there have been reports of systemic toxicity in small pre-term infants exposed to 6 drops of 1% cyclopentolate or 10% phenylephrine. The examiner must also remember that all ophthalmic solutions must be sterile. Pupillary dilation should not be attempted until after the pupil size and appropriate pupillary response in the neurological evaluation have been determined, and the eyelids have been checked for ptosis. No infant with acutely changing CNS disease or with large corneas should have his eyes dilated. Finally, because there is a small risk associated with the use of mydriatics, the examiner must decide what he is searching for and whether it warrants dilating the pupils. For example, if the pupil size is 3 mm and the lens diameter is 6.5 mm, only the central 21% of the lens will be seen. Perhaps some recently formed cortical cataract may not be seen. The risk, then, of missing significant ocular pathology by omitting pupillary dilation in the healthy newborn, though small, *is* present when the eye examination described below is followed. We feel, however, that this exam is practical as a routine.

The equipment necessary consists of a direct, hand-held ophthalmo-scope and a source of bright light (the best type is an otoscope head with light-conducting fibers). Dry 2 × 2 gauze pads and an assistant are definite aids.

The types of ocular abnormalities that are being sought include:

1. recognizable patterns of systemic congenital malformation involving the eyes
2. trauma
3. abnormality of sympathetic innervations of the eye
4. strabismus
5. acute superficial infections
6. lacrimal duct obstruction
7. corneal opacities
8. cataracts
9. retinal lesions

Vision and extraocular muscles are tested as part of the neurological evaluation (see Chapter 4).

The following definitions are given as reminders:

Coloboma—a defect in development (closure of some portion of the eye or its lid);

Epicanthal fold—a fold or extension of skin overlying and partially obscuring the inner canthus;

Interpupillary distance—the distance between the centers of each pupil;

Palpebral width—width of the eyelid margin;

Inner canthus—the medial angle of the eye (the margin between mucous membrane and nasal epidermis);

Outer canthus—the outer angle of the eye;

Palpebral fissure—the elliptical space when the eyelids are normally opened;

Ptosis—an upper lid margin (in a normally opened eye) in the position of primary gaze, which is lower than the point midway between the pupil and the upper margin of the cornea;

Proptosis—(exophthalmus) the forward displaced eye;

Synophrys—an abnormal extension of the eyebrows so that they meet in the midline;

Mongoloid slant—an outer canthus pronouncedly higher than the inner canthus (note that normally the outer canthus is slightly higher than the inner canthus in black and Caucasian babies);

Antimongoloid slant—the inner canthus pronouncedly higher than the outer canthus;

Bulbar conjunctiva—the visible sclera of the eye (the "sclera" loosely refers to that portion that comprises the bulbar conjunctiva);

Heterochromia—dissimilarity in pigmentation between the two irises; and

Strabismus—(squint) the deviation of one or both of the eyes from a point of focus.

The first part of the examination is a careful appraisal of the external features of the eyes in relation to the face and to each other. Normal dimensions are listed in Table 9-1 for reference only. These dimensions are not usually measured in the course of the physical examination. It is generally sufficient to compare the baby with others in the nursery of approximately the same age.

In the external appraisal, the size of the eyes is noted, as is the angle of the line drawn between the inner and outer canthus. If an epicanthal fold is present it is noted, along with the presence and distribution of the eyebrows. Interpupillary distance is observed. The size of the eye and its relation to its orbit are noted.

If distinct abberrations are found in the relationship of the eyes to the face, a careful search must be made for other associated anomalies, which may help to establish the presence of some underlying dysmorphic syndrome. Dr. D. W. Smith's monograph (Smith, 1970) should be consulted for the essential fine points in the differential diagnosis of dysmorphic syndromes involving the eye.

While the baby is in state A-1 or A-3 the eyelids are examined (see Chapter 5), for the presence of ptosis, edema, or signs of trauma. The lid margins are inspected for the usual slightly outward orientation of the single row of lashes. Capillary hemangiomas are frequently seen over the eyelid. To observe the eyes open in their normal position, it is necessary to hold the baby vertically in a dimly lit room.

The lacrimal ducts open through small puncta at the medial aspect of the upper and lower lids. Lacrimal duct obstruction is not uncommon in newborns; however, since tear production is not usually well

Table 9-1.   External features of the newborn eye

Normal Dimensions	Full-Term Newborn (range)
Interpupillary distance	39 mm (33–46 mm)
Inner canthal distance	20 ± 4 mm (13–26 mm)
Anterior/posterior diameter of eye	16.5 mm
Palpebral width	17–27 mm
Pupil size	2–4 mm
Cornea	9–10 mm

established until 3–4 weeks of postnatal life, the best clue to this problem, excessive tearing, may not be obvious. If the duct is thought to be obstructed, the lacrimal sac should be palpated. If material is discharged from the puncta, the obstruction probably lies in the nasal communication.

The conjunctivae are inspected for the presence of exudate, vasodilation, erythema, edema, jaundice, and hemorrhages. Silver nitrate prophylaxis may cause a chemical irritation of the eye, which is apparent during the first days of life. The lid may be edematous, and there may be a proteinaceous sterile exudate and vasodilation of the conjunctival vessels. This form of conjunctivitis spontaneously resolves by the third to fourth day of life. It is very common, may be unilateral, and is generally of great concern to parents, although it is benign. Infectious conjunctivitis is rarely noted on the first day of life, and is accompanied by a purulent discharge from which the causative organism may be cultured. Very rarely, gonococcal conjunctivitis may be acquired after birth. Inclusion blennorrhea due to chlamydia begins 7 to 10 days after delivery. Small scleral hemorrhages are commonly seen after normal deliveries. The sclerae of most full-term infants are white. Pre-term infants have very thin sclerae, which may appear bluish. *Distinctly* blue sclera are abnormal in the full-term newborn and suggest possible connective tissue dysgenesis (such as osteogenesis imperfecta or cutis laxa).

Pupils should be equal, and should react to bright light with consensual constriction. A unilateral small pupil and ptosis of the same eye suggest a lesion of the cervical sympathetic chain. If a lesion is the cause of this finding, an absence of sweating on the same side of the face will also be noted. The pupillary light reflex is entirely subcortical and its presence does not rule out cortical blindness.

Testing extraocular movement is described in the chapter on the nervous system (Chapter 4). The iris is normally incompletely pigmented for the first six months of life. The normal Caucasian newborn infant's iris is blue or blue-grey for the first few months of life; the dark-skinned Caucasian infant and babies of other races may have pigmented irises at birth or soon after.

Heterochromia (different colors between eyes or in the same eye) should be noted if present; it may indicate the later development of renal neoplasia. The presence of a coloboma should be sought. The coloboma may make the pupil look like a keyhole, and it, too, is frequently associated with abnormalities in other organ systems (Smith, 1970).

The cornea is now closely inspected using a point source of bright light (otoscope head) cast tangentially across the eye from the temporal side. Any cloudiness is noted. The normal cornea is shining and glassy, but the pre-term infant may occasionally have a transitory haziness for the first week. If there is excessive tearing or photophobia in the absence of conjunctivitis, the corneal diameter should be measured. A corneal diameter of 12–13 mm raises the suspicion of congenital glaucoma.

The lens is next inspected for cataracts with a bright light held 6 to 8 inches from the eye. The +10 diopter ophthlmoscope lens is appropriate. The normal newborn's lens transmits a clear red color back to the observer: this phenomenon is known as the "red reflex." If cataracts are present, the red image of the fundus is interrupted by black opacities that represent the cataracts. Again, one must remember that the pupil size determines the area of the lens that can be inspected. About 3% of term infants still may have remnants of the hyaloid artery. These remnants appear as thin strands reaching from the retina to the lens.

Good visualization of the ocular fundus is difficult through the undilated pupil of an agitated infant. However, even without pupillary dilation, we may be successful if the eye exam is performed near the beginning of the physical examination when the infant is still content and quiet. The retina is best visualized in a dimly lit room since the pupil will tend to be more dilated. The infant will also be more apt to keep his eyes open spontaneously if he is in a vertical or semivertical position. The fundus viewed through a +1 to +3 diopter lens appears as a flat surface. The retina is nearly transparent and its surface glistens. The color of the fundus in the newborn is normally reddish pink and the optic nerve may appear pale, but its margins should be sharp. The macula may be indistinct in the pre-term infant, but in the full-term infant it should have a reddish brown color. It is located about 1½ disc diameters temporal to the disc. Isolated retinal hemorrhages may commonly be seen in the fullterm newborn and have little significance. They are probably related to the rigors of labor and delivery. The normal retina has no demarcated pigmented or depigmented areas, and is decreasingly vascularized as one approaches the temporal periphery. The blood vessels should not be tortuous or appear to anastamose.

To review: the infant should be content at the outset of the examination. This usually means that the eye inspection should be one of the first steps of the physical examination to be performed. The infant is held in a vertical (or semi-vertical) position so that the eyes remain open and the face and eyes can be quickly inspected. Measurements are made only when indicated by history or other findings. The lids and conjunctivae are inspected and a bright light is focused tangentially across the pupil. Pupillary responses are checked and the red reflex is sought; finally, the retina is examined. When performed as indicated, the examination of the eye takes no more than 5 minutes.

LITERATURE CITED

Adler, M. 1962. Textbook of Ophthalmology. W. B. Saunders Company, Philadelphia.

Read, J. E., and M. F. Goldberg. 1977. Diseases of the Eye. In: R. E. Behrman (ed.), Neonatal-Perinatal Medicine. C. V. Mosby Company, St. Louis.

Smith, D. W. 1970. Recognizable Patterns of Human Malformation. 1st Ed. W. B. Saunders Company, Philadelphia.

10 / EXAMINATION OF THE CHEST AND LUNGS

The chest examination for the newborn includes evaluation of both soft and bony thoracic tissues, the lungs, and the heart. Inspection, percussion, palpation, and auscultation are employed. The cardiac exam is discussed in the next chapter.

THORACIC TISSUES

The assessment of the soft and bony thoracic tissues begins with an inspection of the size and shape of the thoracic cage. Chest circumference and internipple distance are measured. The average chest circumference of a normal, full-term infant is about 33 ± 3 cm; approximately 2 cm smaller than the normal head circumference. This difference is greatest at about 32 weeks gestation. If the head circumference is greater than that of the chest, intrauterine growth retardation is suggested. Microcephaly is suspected if the head's circumference is less than that of the chest. The internipple distance in the full-term newborn averages about 25% of the total chest circumference.

The sternum and ribs are palpated for asymmetry in their contour and number, or for any masses and/or crepitance. This latter finding indicates subcutaneous air, usually from a pulmonary airleak. A small, sharp, cartilaginous mass, the xiphoid process, is felt at the inferior end of the hard bony sternum in the newborn (mothers are often alarmed by this normal finding).

Breasts and nipples are inspected for their number, symmetry, size, color, turgor, and discharge. Supernumerary nipples are found in a line verticle to the main nipple on the right or left side, usually appearing as small, rasied, pigmented areas. The full-term newborn has a stippled areola with a raised edge and a diameter of at least 0.75 cm. Breast tissue should be palpable on both sides, with at least one breast having a diameter greater than 1 cm. Breast size, shape, and configuration are helpful in gestational age assessment (Chapter 2). Hypertrophy of the breast is seen in a small percentage of newborns: a milky discharge from the breast is an uncommon but normal finding. Both of these resolve with time, the hypertrophy more gradually. Erythema is sometimes observed in the breast area, and inspection of other parts of the skin help to differentiate inflammation from a normal rash. Infrequently, the neonatal breasts may become infected (mastitis).

LUNGS

Normal physical findings in the pulmonary exam of the newborn are quite variable, being influenced by the time after birth when the exam is performed, the pattern of respiration during the exam, the sleep-wake status of the baby, when the baby was fed, maternal drugs taken prior to delivery, and the physical environment. Skin color, as a component of the pulmonary exam, provides information about tissue oxygenation. Cyanosis is addressed in the sections dealing with skin (Chapter 6) and cardiovascular evaluations (Chapter 11), as well as the final chapter on diagnostic considerations (Chapter 14). Obviously, the presence of cyanosis is an important diagnostic finding.

Respiratory rate is counted for one full minute. Normally, the newborn's respiratory rate is approximately 40 per minute, but there is considerable variability. The rate normally reaches a peak by 10 minutes after birth then gradually decreases during the next hours of life. A persistently elevated rate is abnormal, but the respiratory rate will fluctuate widely. Repeated examinations will decide whether a normal trend has been established (Desmond et al., 1963).

Environmental temperature should be recorded at the time of the examination because extremes in temperature can inhibit or accelerate the respiratory rate. Consequently, hyper- or hypothermia will produce tachypnea or apnea. Babies born by cesarean section normally have a higher average respiratory rate during the first four to six hours of life than those born by vaginal delivery. This may be related to delayed pulmonary fluid disappearance in the CS group.

Irregularities in respiratory patterns occur in all newborn infants, increasingly so in the more premature. When the pattern is characterized by a ventilatory burst, followed by an apneic period of 5 to 15 seconds repetitively, it is called "periodic breathing." During the ventilatory phase of periodic breathing, the respiratory rate may be 50 to 60 per minute. In normal infants periodic breathing is more commonly found at higher altitudes. Follow-up examination later in the neonatal period for a full-term newborn will normally show decreasing evidence of periodic breathing. In the premature baby, periodic breathing is noted intermittently until at least 36 weeks post-conceptual age, regardless of when the baby is born. More prolonged periods of apnea may be termed "apneic spells," especially when associated with bradycardia. The bradycardia implies a cardiovascular response to asphyxia and is an ominous finding.

Respiratory patterns are significantly influenced by the state of consciousness (see Chapter 5). Deep sleep is associated with a fairly regular breathing pattern, and rapid eye movement (REM) sleep, with periodic breathing. The awake states are typified by grossly irregular breathing associated with muscle movement, sucking, and crying. Inspiratory gasps are frequent. Often, a second inspiration is superimposed on the first.

Next, the symmetry and expansion of the chest is observed. Although this is usually not objectively measured during the routine exam, hypo- or hyperventilation is easily discerned by observing chest expansion. Asymmetry of expansion is an abnormal finding and provides a clue to such congenital problems as diaphragmatic hernia and pneumothorax.

The respiratory muscles are observed next. The newborn normally uses his diaphragm for breathing, then gradually adapts to greater intercostal muscle use as he ages. Under abnormal conditions, the newborn will use more abdominal musculature to accomplish respiration. This is observed as a "see-saw" breathing pattern because the abdomen and chest move asynchronously up and down.

In order to provide a semi-quantitative observation of a newborn's overall respiratory status, Silverman and Andersen (Silverman and Andersen, 1956) introduced an index of respiratory distress which has become a universal standard. The index is determined by grading each of five criteria: *chest lag, intercostal retraction, xiphoid retraction, nasal dilation*, and *expiratory grunt*. This index is a dynamic measure used to assess the progress of a newborn's respiratory status. It should be recorded for every infant with tachypnea or any other suspected respiratory problem.

Percussion of the chest is not commonly done in the routine physical because of the baby's small chest size in relation to the large fingers of the examiner. Auscultation of the lungs should be done with a warm

Table 10-1. Assessment of respiratory function by physical examination in the newborn

Observable Criteria	Score		
	0	1	2
Chest lag	synchronized movement	lag on inspiration	asynchronous see-saw breathing
Intercostal retractions	no retractions	minimal	marked
Xiphoid retraction	no retraction	minimal	marked
Expiratory grunt	none heard	heard only with stethoscope	heard with ear
Dilation of nares	none seen	minimal	minimal

After Silverman and Andersen (1956).

stethoscope that has a small diaphragm and a bell no larger than 2 cm in diameter, again because of the reduced area to be examined. Also because of size constraints, localization of auscultated sound is less reliable in the newborn than in the older patient.

The best time for auscultation is while the baby is quiet. Posture may also influence auscultatory findings because babies who consistently lie in one position aerate certain areas of the lung less well than others. The examination in the first minutes and hours of life usually reveals rales and rhonchi in the chest due to the presence of fetal fluid: reabsorption of this fluid is associated with improved auscultation.

Differences in auscultatory findings between upper and lower parts of the chest, anterior and posterior, and right and left sides need to be recorded. As with observation of chest exapansion, such findings suggest localized areas of lung collapse. If breath sounds from an area of the lungs cannot be detected, transillumination for an air leak as well as AP and lateral chest x-rays are indicated.

Excessive movement and/or crying by the infant are the most common causes for an inadequate pulmonary auscultation. Other noises that confuse the interpretation of pulmonary findings may be generated from the proximal gastrointestinal tract and from the upper airway. Movement of the stethoscope to those areas will often determine the origin of such adventitious sounds. When the examiner hears a wheeze in the newborn's chest, the nose and throat are auscultated to eliminate the possibility of partial upper airway obstruction. Bubbling gastrointestinal sounds may be heard in the chest even when the esophagus and stomach are normally located, or when a diaphragmatic defect has allowed bowel egress to the thoracic cavity. Other findings help to distinguish auscultated sounds (Chapter 3).

Transillumination as an adjunct to the physical exam of the pulmonary system in the newborn has been developed by Kuhns et al. (1975). A high-intensity light, transmitted via a fiberoptic probe, has been adapted for neonatal use by placing a piece of soft, black rubber sheep-nipple over the tip (Scanlon, 1977). The probe is placed on different areas of the chest and the amount of transillumination noted. Particular attention is paid to the comparison of upper to lower and right to left sides of the chest while the baby is supine. Free intrathoracic air is readily observed since there is a distinct asymmetrical hyperlucency.

LITERATURE CITED

Desmond, M. M., R. R. Franklin, C. Valbona, R. M. Hill, R. Plumb, H. Arnold, and T. Watts. 1963. The clinical behavior of the newly born. J. Pediatr. 62:307.

Kuhns, L. R., F. J. Rednarek, M. L. Wyman, D. W. Roloff, and R. C. Borer. 1975. Diagnosis of pneumothorax or pneumomediastinum in the neonate by transillumination.

Scanlon, J. W. 1977. Modifications of chest transillumination. Pediatrics 60:766.

Silverman, W. A., and D. H. Andersen. 1956. A controlled clinical trial of effects of water mist on obstructive respiratory signs, death rates and necropsy findings among premature infants. Pediatrics 17:1.

11 / EXAMINATION OF THE CARDIOVASCULAR SYSTEM

The physical examination of the cardiovascular system in the newborn is complex because of a number of intrinsic and extrinsic factors that cause normal findings to change during the initial hours and days of life.

The intrinsic influences are a rapidly altering cardiac function plus a reactive, changing, systemic and pulmonary vascular capacitance and resistance. Gestational age, time after birth, and the baby's behavioral state are important considerations when interpreting the cardiovascular system.

Extrinsic influences include environment, temperature, any cardiotonic drugs to which the fetus/baby has been exposed,[1] and any other type of outside stimulus, such as touch, sound, and light. To best understand the physiologic cardiovascular changes in the newborn that are reflected in the physical exam, this assessment should ideally be performed directly after birth, again within 6 hours, at the end of the first day, and on the third day of life. However, for the full-term, low-risk, asymptomatic neonate, the *minimal* routine would be an exam on day 1 and on day 3 of life.

Completion of the cardiovascular exam includes assessment of such systems as the skin and subcutaneous tissue, liver, spleen, and lungs. Pertinent relationships will only be touched on lightly in this chapter and are discussed in more detail in appropriate chapters.

The cardiovascular examination begins with noting the color of the infant's skin and mucous membranes. The four important color observations here are *blue* (cyanosis), *white* (pallor), *purple* (plethora), or *pink* (normal). In darkly pigmented babies more attention is given to less pigmented areas (the tongue, gingiva, and nailbeds). The intensity and quality of the light in the examining area obviously influence these findings. The use of blue-light phototherapy, for example, makes dermal color observations difficult.

If cyanosis is present, the somatic distribution is recorded. The effect of crying on the depth of cyanosis and its recovery over time must be carefully noted. Forced expiration, as in crying, facilitates extrapulmonic shunting by increasing intrapulmonary pressure

---

[1] These include almost all obstetrical analgesic/anesthetic agents, as well as more widely recognized "heart medicines."

transiently. Cyanosis of the distal extremities ("peripheral cyanosis") or cyanosis confined to the face and scalp (acryocyanosis) are normal findings in the newborn during the first hours of life. Cyanosis of the mucous membranes during crying in the first few hours after birth may be normal as well, but is worrisome and *must* be re-evaluated. If cyanosis persists, a more complete evaluation including blood gas studies, electrocardiogram, chest x-ray, and cardiology consultation should be done. It is important to remember that the differential diagnosis of cyanosis is not confined to the cardiovascular system; primary intracranial or pulmonary pathology may be responsible.

If pallor is present, the distribution over the body is noted. If there is generalized pallor, peripheral vasoconstriction, acute cardiac failure, and lack of adequate circulating hemoglobin (anemia) are prominent concerns. Pallor may be disguised by the presence of other skin colors due to cyanosis or jaundice. The most subjective part of the newborn's skin observation is the measurement of "pinkness." Although pinkness usually reflects skin opacity and pigmentation, some qualitative assessment of circulating blood volume may be inferred from the intensity of the pink color. A purplish coloration of the skin may result from a combination of saturated and unsaturated hemoglobin. This finding occurs in neonatal plethora, a condition associated occasionally with both cardiopulmonary and neurological findings. It can be a real masquerade!

After noting its color, palpate the infant's skin for temperature, moisture, turgor, and capillary filling time.

The distal extremities may normally be cooler to palpation than the rest of the body during the initial hours of life. A *repeated* finding of extremity temperature difference, despite normal environmental and core temperatures, is abnormal. Sweating is not a usual finding in the newborn. If sweating is present despite a normal environmental temperature, congestive heart failure or drug withdrawal should be considered. Edema of the dorsum of the feet and hands is not normal in the full-term newborn, but can be seen at some time in almost all premature babies of less than 2,000 g in birthweight. Isolated pedal edema in the full-term infant is a hallmark of Turner's syndrome (XO chromosome), and will usually disappear unexplainedly.

Capillary filling time is assessed by depressing the baby's skin, preferably over one central and one peripheral area. After blanching the skin, the time required for the return to the normal skin color is noted. Capillary filling time of greater than 3 seconds is probably abnormal. The examiner should use his own capillary filling time as a comparison (provided the examiner is neither vasoconstricted nor peripherally dilated). The difference in filling times between central and peripheral sites is noted.

Respiratory activity is observed in relationship to the cardiovascular exam. Respiratory rate and effort are recorded serially as discussed in Chapter 10. The liver and the spleen are examined for their size and consistency as described in Chapter 12. A large, soft liver with a poorly defined edge may result from congestive heart failure. Note that the liver, used as a venous pressure "bag," is a sensitive indicator of elevated right atrial pressure. Serial weights also contribute to the cardiovascular exam since abrupt changes in weight must reflect fluid fluxes and, thus, cardiovascular function.

The pulses are examined next. This is best accomplished with the baby quiet, in a resting state. The jugular venous pulse of the newborn is best evaluated with the head turned to the side opposite the pulse to be observed. The atrial (*a*) and ventricular (*v*) waves of the jugular pulse can be recognized in the sleeping newborn. The *a* wave is produced by atrial contraction in end diastole (presystole). The *v* wave reflects the end of ventricular systole and gradual right atrial filling from the systemic return. A prominent jugular venous pulse wave may be normally seen in the first few hours of life, particularly in those babies who received a large placental transfusion at birth.

The arterial pulses are now examined. Again, the best assessment is conducted while the baby is warm and relaxed. The examiner's thumbs are theoretically the most accurate for pulse palpation because of their greater number of tactile receptors; however, intrinsic pulsation in the thumbs may create confusion. We suggest using the index fingers for pulse evaluation. The presence or the absence of pulses and their amplitude and symmetry, and the quality of the pulse's rise and fall, are the criteria for arterial pulse evaluation. Frequency of pulsation is discussed in the section on heart rate. The pedal pulses are examined bilaterally. These are not always felt in the newborn, so their absence on palpation is not necessarily abnormal. Palpation is done over both femoral areas. Absence of detectable pulses in the femoral area is abnormal and indicates inadequate aortic blood flow. Here it is important to note symmetry. The brachial pulses are palpated bilaterally and should be felt easily. A comparison should also be made between the brachial and femoral pulses. Knowing the postnatal age is important in arterial pulse examination because hyperdynamic pulses are usual in the first several hours of life, but uncommon (and perhaps pathological) on the second or third day.

The systemic blood pressure (BP) should be taken in every newborn. This is done with the baby in a quiet state. The current methods of indirect blood pressure determination in the newborn use either peripheral pulse detection, arterial inflow detection, or detection of artery wall motion. Detection of the peripheral pulse distal to the occluding

Table 11-1.   Upper and lower limits for blood pressures (mm hg) on the first day of life

	Birthweight (kg)				
Blood pressure	1.0–1.5	1.5–2.0	2.0–2.5	2.5–3.0	3.0–4.5
Systolic	40–55	45–60˙	50–65	55–70	60–80
Diastolic[a]	20–30	23–35	27–38	31–45	35–55

[a] The range for diastolic blood pressures in the newborn is less well established than that for systolic.

extremity cuff is reliable for detecting systolic pressure only. The real measurement problems stem from the influences of respiratory variation and the cuff size. The examiner should use a cuff with a width of about one-third to one-half of the circumference of the occluded extremity. Too small a cuff falsely elevates the reading. In the full-term newborn, a cuff width of 2.5 to 3.0 cm is usually appropriate. The best method of routine indirect systolic and diastolic blood pressure determination in the newborn appears to be artery wall motion detection. The pulse sensor is connected to a Doppler ultrasonic transducer for amplification. The rushing pulse sound is easily heard. This technique is more reliable then either arterial inflow (flush) inspection, or palpation and auscultation of the distal pulse. The Doppler method can also estimate diastolic pressure in a crude way.

Body weight, gestational age, and postnatal age are the important determinants of blood pressure magnitude. As a very general rule, the newborn weighing more than 3 kg has a mean BP of 50 mm Hg; from 2 to 3 kg, 43 mm Hg; and from 1 to 2 kg, 38 mm Hg (Kitterman et al., 1969; Paxson, 1978). Further details of age and weight variations in the range of normal pressures may be seen in Table 11-1.

These figures are based on measurements taken on the first day. With regard to postnatal age (PA), the systolic pressure falls after birth, reaches a minimum at 3 hours of age, and then rises to reach a plateau at approximately 4 to 6 days at a level close to the initial postpartum level. Diastolic pressure usually does not fall, but gradually begins to rise at around two days. A formula that takes into account the BW (kg), GA (weeks), and PA (hours) has been derived and approximates the systolic blood pressure (Bucci et al., 1972):

$$BP = 23.2 + 8.1\ BW + 0.50\ GA + 0.23\ PA - 0.0016\ (PA)^2$$

If there is no standard chart available, the examiner may wish to use this computation even though it is cumbersome. The formula is useful between 3 and 96 hours of age. Repeated findings outside the normal range need further investigation. The full-term infant's limits usually are obtained during the first week of life. Data are less clear for the pre-term baby after day 1.

If there are technical difficulties in obtaining blood pressure measurements in the arms, or abnormal pulses are found in the legs, blood pressure should be measured in the lower extremities. Lower extremity blood pressure is slightly higher than in the arms. An increase or widening of the pulse pressure (defined as the difference between systolic and diastolic values) may be pathological, and may indicate pulse pressure "run-off" (as in a patent ductus or aortic insufficiency).

The precordium is examined next. Inspection of the precordium often reveals hyperactivity during the initial hours of life, but it subsequently decreases. In some premature infants, precordial activity is visible at all times because of thin skin and the small amount of subcutaneous tissue. Percussion is of limited use in the newborn precordial examination. Palpation of the precordium is initiated by localizing the point of maximal impulse (PMI) using a single finger placed on the chest. The PMI is usually found on the left side in the fourth to fifth intercostal space, just medial to the mid-clavicular line. In the initial hours of life, the PMI may be found farther to the right, even substernally, representing normal right ventricular activity. It is important to palpate across the entire anterior chest, because the PMI can be shifted either by a congenital or acquired acute intrathoracic problem, such as tension pneumothorax (see Chapters 10 and 14). In babies with a risk of mediastinal shift from pneumothorax, a small piece of tape with a marking is left over the PMI to facilitate repeat comparison.

It is also important to evaluate the strength of the PMI. Similar to inspection, precordial palpation in the initial newborn exam normally reveals increased activity, and may even be characterized by a thrill. This will disappear after the first several hours. Heaves, lifts, thrusts, and thrills that are noticed on palpation should be recorded. Since the right ventricle is predominant in the full-term newborn and is anteriorly located, physical findings should be interpreted with this in mind. In some normal babies, closure of the pulmonary valve may be palpable over the second intercostal space to the left of the sternum, especially where there is little skin and subcutaneous tissue.

Auscultation of the heart is performed next. Clearly, the infant should be quiet and inactive. Heart rate (HR) is counted over a full minute's time because of considerable variability in this measure in the same infant. Heart rate is affected by gestational age, postnatal age, sleep-wake state, feeding, and physical environment. The average resting heart rate in the full-term newborn starts at 160/min directly after birth, then decreases until about 3 hours of age, when the mean is 130/min. HR then plateaus until the end of the first 24 hours, then slowly rises to 140/min by seven days of life (Rowe and Mehrizi, 1968).

There is considerable variation in HR among babies. Any resting heart rate from 110 to 160 is not considered abnormal; however, the examiner must remember that since HR variation is normal, metronomically fixed heart rate is clearly aberrant.

The rhythm of the heartbeat is noted next. Because of the relatively fast heartbeat in the newborn, it may be difficult to detect abnormalities of rhythm on the physical exam. Paradoxically, the newborn is more likely to have abnormalities of rate and rhythm than is an older child. Brief episodes of cardiac deceleration are often observed in the full-term newborn, followed by rebound acceleration. Episodic bradycardia has been found as frequently as once per hour in 30% of full-term infants. Such episodes are much more frequent among premature babies (Valimaki and Tarlo, 1971). The frequency of marked sinus bradycardia correlates inversely with gestational age. Atrioventricular block, atrial and ventricular premature contractions, and sinus arrest are also found more commonly in the premature newborn. Such occurrences necessitate the use of continuous electronic HR monitoring. The examiner should also attempt to quantify the frequency of "missed beats" per unit time and determine whether an abnormal rhythm is regular or irregular in its periodicity. Abnormal rhythm induced by vagal stimulation will decrease as gestational and postnatal age increase.

The evaluation of heart sounds by auscultation is made difficult by the rapid heart rate of the newborn. The first heart sound is usually loud at birth. An early systolic ejection sound is best detected during the first few hours after birth at the lower left sternal border. The second sound is loud and single at birth. About 4 hours after delivery, detectable splitting of this sound is noted in approximately 50% of normal full-term infants. An easily detectable split can be heard in two-thirds of infants by 16 hours, and in four-fifths by 48 hours. Third and fourth sounds are rarely heard at this age.

Murmurs are heard frequently during the neonatal period, particularly during the first day or two of life. During the first 48 hours a majority of normal newborns have detectable murmurs that are not pathological. Most common (heard in almost 60%) are systolic ejection murmurs of a vibrating quality in the second left intercostal space of grade 1 or 2/6 intensity. Less frequently, a systolic murmur (either continuous or crescendo) is heard in healthy full-term infants, especially those between 4 and 6 hours of age. This sound may be explained by dropping pulmonary vascular resistance and/or changing flow through the ductus arteriosus.

Heart murmurs that occur or persist after the first two days of life are less frequent and require further evaluation, such as a chest x-ray, electrocardiogram, echocardiogram, or cardiology consultation. Murmurs due to left-to-right shunts may not appear until the third day because of the normal decrease in pulmonary vascular resistance at this time (see Chapter 14). As in any age group, a murmur should be described by its intensity, quality, shape, location, and radiation. It may also be helpful to press the liver superiorly while listening to the murmur and note any change in auscultatory findings. Such a maneuver produces an increase in right atrial pressure. This may cause a left-to-right shunt to disappear momentarily, or to increase an existing right-to-left shunt. Finally, in those babies with physical signs of cardiovascular pathology, particularly with congestive heart failure, auscultation of the cranium and abdomen is necessary to detect bruits, which indicate the presence of arteriovenous malformation.

Remember, continued practice, diligence, and concentration in listening to the neonate's heart will reward the examiner by rapidly developing his cardiac diagnostic skills!

LITERATURE CITED

Bucci, G., L. Piccanato, A. Scalamandol, P. G. Sovignoni, M. Mendicini, E. Casagrande, and S. P. Bucci. 1972. The systemic systolic blood pressure of newborns with low birth weight. Acta. Paediatr. Scand. 229 (Suppl.):5–26.

Kitterman, J. A., R. H. Phibbs, and W. H. Tooley. 1969. Aortic blood pressure in normal newborn infants during the first 12 hours of life. Pediatrics 44:959.

Paxson, C. L. 1978. Neonatal shock in the first postnatal day. Am. J. Dis. Child. 132:509.

Rowe, R. D., and A. Mehrizi. 1968. The Neonate with Congenital Heart Disease, Ch. 3. W. B. Sunders Company, Philadelphia.

Smith, C. A., and N. M. Nelson. 1976. The Physiology of the Newborn Infant. Ch. 4. 4th Ed. Charles C Thomas, Publisher, Springfield, Ill.

Valimaki, I., and P. A. Tarlo. 1971. Heart rate patterns and apnea in newborn infants. Am. J. Obstet. Gynecol. 110:343.

12 / EXAMINATION OF THE ABDOMEN

INSPECTION

The abdomen of the normal full-term newborn is soft, symmetrical, slightly rounded, and moves synchronously with the chest in respiration. In the premature infants, however, the abdomen often appears distended because of poor muscle tone.

A flat, flabby, "pancake" abdomen is abnormal and most commonly is associated with decreased muscle tone in an infant compromised either by drug or neurological depression. Rarely, the reason may be the congenital absence of the abdominal musculature, called the "prune-belly" syndrome. This syndrome occurs chiefly in males and is associated with a high incidence of urinary tract abnormalities.

Persistent abdominal distension is a reliable (though nonspecific) sign of disease in the newborn. It is due either to enlargement of a solid abdominal organ, or to bowel dilation from obstruction or infection. The presence of visible peristalsis in a distended abdomen alerts the observer to the possibility of obstruction. For example, visible left upper-quadrant distension and peristalsis suggests pyloric or duodenal obstruction, particularly in a vomiting neonate.

The umbilical cord, protruding from the midpoint of the abdomen, is normally pearly white and gelatinous at birth. It becomes dark and shriveled as it dries and falls off between 10 and 14 days.

Occasionally, a small, red, raw-appearing granuloma will form at the site of the separation of the umbilical cord. The term *umbilical polyp* is used for this superficial low-grade infection.

The two arteries of the freshly cut stump are clearly seen as retracted, thick white cords, whereas the single vein is thin-walled and splayed open, often with a small dark clot in its lumen. The presence of only one umbilical artery should be noted, as it may be associated with other congenital malformations (commonly urinary).

The thickness of the cord stump relative to the quantity of Wharton's jelly serves as an indicator of the nutritional status of the fetus, now a newborn. A thick cord is seen more frequently in the "large-for-dates" infant, while a small thin cord is most common in undernourished "light-for-dates" neonates. Green discoloration of the cord is a sign that meconium was passed in utero twelve hours or more before delivery.

A palpable gap between the two rectus muscles is common in the healthy neonate and swelling may be visible with crying in such "diastasis recti." An umbilical hernia may also be felt and, occasionally, seen. This finding, benign in the newborn, is more common in black babies. The great majority spontaneously reduce by 2 years of age.

The umbilical hernia and supraumbilical rectus swelling should be distinguished from the much less common epigastric hernia, which is a palpable, firm, mid-line nodule located between the umbilicus and the inferior end of the sternum. The nodule consists of a small, irreducible protrusion of fat through the midline. Occasionally, a small knuckle of peritoneum may also protrude. Such a lesion, when palpated, usually elicits an expression of pain from the baby. These defects require surgical consultation.

The very rare patent vitello-intestinal duct may be noted in the umbilical area. This may be seen as an opening in the cord that discharges fluid or, less commonly, feces. It requires prompt surgical intervention, since bowel obstruction may result from intestinal kinking or prolapse around the duct.

Next, the abdomen should be palpated. To allow adequate palpation, the infant must be quiet and relaxed to reduce voluntary muscle tone. The examiner first defines the liver margin, then places the palmar surface of his right index finger parallel to the right costal margin just above the groin. While applying gentle pressure, the examiner gradually advances the examining finger proximally until the liver edge slips below his exploring finger. This is normally about 1–2 cm inferior to the costal margin. The anterior-inferior edge of the liver is then felt. The normal liver edge is sharp; when rounded, it suggests congestion and may be an early, valuable sign of congestive heart failure, especially when cardiac and respiratory findings are consistent.

Next, the consistency of the liver is determined by palpating its anterior surface. It is usually firm. A very hard or nodular surface is abnormal. Occasionally, respiratory disease with chest hyperexpansion will cause the liver edge to be lower than normal and feel large. This phenomenon may also occur with the spleen, although it is smaller.

A similar technique is used to palpate the spleen on the left side, although in the majority of infants only the splenic tip is felt. The presence of a palpable spleen more than 1 cm below the left costal margin suggests enlargement and warrants further investigation. In infants with certain congenital heart defects the spleen may be absent and, therefore, unpalpable.

The remainder of the abdomen is then gently palpated for abnormal masses. Cystic or solid-feeling masses are most frequently of urinary tract origin. Malignant tumors are most uncommon in the newborn. Examination of the kidneys and bladder is often done during the abdominal examination. This subject is discussed in detail in Chapter 13.

The examiner should remember to watch the infant for pain when gently palpating the abdomen. Even a very sick newborn who has serious intestinal pathology will respond to palpation by crying, grimacing, or involuntarily contracting his abdominal muscles.

The next step is auscultation. The presence or absence of bowel sounds and their quality and intensity should be noted. These findings must be interpreted in the light of other abdominal findings and the clinical history. Hyperdynamic bowel sounds soon after feeding in a well infant with a soft abdomen may be normal, whereas the same bowel sounds in a vomiting infant with a distended abdomen suggest obstruction. Transmitted breath sounds may be heard over the upper abdomen, particularly the stomach.

The lumbar areas are palpated for masses, and auscultated for the presence of renal bruits, which are a sign of renal artery stenosis, although such findings are very rare.

Transillumination is not part of the usual abdominal examination; however, in the presence of distension or organomegaly, this technique may be helpful to define intraperitoneal air or fluid, or to determine the nature of cystic masses within the abdominal cavity.

The groins should be examined by inspection and palpation in both the relaxed and crying states. The groins are flat and it is not uncommon to see normal pulsations of the femoral arteries in thin full-term infants and in premature infants. The femoral arteries must always be palpated. Absence of the arterial pulse may be an early sign of coarctation of the aorta. Such a finding should be pursued by measuring the blood pressure in the lower limbs. In significant coarctation the pressure differential between limbs and legs will be considerable.

The character of the femoral pulse must be determined. The examiner asks himself, does it feel bounding, weak, thready, or irregular? These pulses should be palpated simultaneously, along with the brachial pulse with which it is comparable in intensity and timing. Significant lag-time between brachial and femoral pulses, as well as decreased femoral pulse intensity, provide further support for a diagnosis of coarctation of the aorta. Bounding femoral pulses, on the other hand, suggest a large left-to-right "run-off." The most common diagnosis in this case is a patent ductus arteriosus. Further discussion of pulses and blood pressure is found in Chapter 11. We obviously feel that this topic is an important one.

When palpating the femoral area remember the mnemonic NAVEL, which represents the sequence of structures from lateral to medial in the femoral triangle: N = nerve, A = artery, V = vein, E = empty space and L = lymph nodes. Knowing this sequence will aid the examiner in diagnosing palpable masses and in locating the femoral artery.

All swellings in the groin are abnormal. In the male infant, groin and scrotum must be palpated simultaneously as incompletely descended or retractile testes are common. Chapter 13 discusses this further. With normal bilaterally descended testes, any observed or felt groin swellings are usually indirect inguinal hernias and/or hydroceles. The slippery feeling of the two peritoneal surfaces sliding over each other in the inguinal canal (the so-called "silk glove sign" so helpful in the older child) is rarely appreciated in the neonate. These swellings may not be seen or palpated when the infant is relaxed, but when present, are most frequently noted when the infant is straining or crying.

Indirect inguinal hernias are less common in female infants, but they do occur. They feel exactly like those of the male, but may also be located in the labia majora. The presence of a groin swelling in the female newborn should also alert the observer to the possibility of an abnormal gonad. Determination of sexual genotype is mandatory before the "hernia" is explored.

The anal area must be carefully inspected for fistulae, the presence of an anus, and the muscle tone quality of the anal sphincter. The introduction of the examiner's pinky is usually sufficient to determine patency of the anus. Any suspicion of an anorectal abnormality warrants prompt pediatric surgical consultation.

13 / EXAMINATION OF THE GENITOURINARY SYSTEM

The complete physical examination of the newborn genitourinary system involves inspection, percussion, palpation, and, occasionally, transillumination. The exam should be conducted when the baby is in a relaxed, quiet state. To adequately evaluate the upper urinary tract, abdominal muscular resistance must be overcome. This is most easily accomplished during the first 48 hours of life, when muscle tone is lowest.

The left kidney is normally felt by placing the right hand beneath the left lumbar region, and exploring the left flank with the thumb (or fingers) of the left hand; this technique is reversed for examination of the right kidney. To detect abnormal placement or orientation of the kidneys, the upper quadrants are palpated, the lumbar vertebral column is felt, and the abdomen is compressed from the sides, allowing the abdominal contents to slip past the fingers. The length of the normal kidney in the full-term newborn is between 4.5 and 5.0 cm from upper to lower poles. The right kidney is normally situated lower than the left. Both are normally located lower in the abdomen than they are in an older child. In addition to size, the kidneys are examined for shape and texture, and careful notation is made of any irregularities. Fetal lobulation is occasionally felt and is normal. Hydronephrosis, cystic kidneys, neoplasia, and hypoplasia may be suspected on the basis of palpatory findings (see Chapter 14). Further evaluation of such suspicions with intravenous pyelography and/or renal scan is requisite.

A modification of the procedure for kidney palpation has been described (Perlman and William, 1976) in which the infant is supine, the upper trunk and occiput are supported, and the hips are individually flexed to relax the abdominal musculature. On the same side as the flexed hip, the fingers of the free examining hand are placed posteriorly on the flank. The thumb is placed on the abdomen and pressed posteriorly to meet the fingers; while maintaining this pressure, the thumb is gently moved up and down, then medially and laterally.

The ureters cannot be palpated in the newborn unless there is abnormal enlargement or dilation. When enlarged, they are appreciated as soft, cylindrical, and compressible intra-abdominal masses. Transillumination reveals their fluid-filled state.

The newborn bladder is best examined by percussion and gentle palpation. Sliding the examining fingers inferiorly from the navel may also be useful. The bladder is narrower and found relatively higher in the abdomen than it is in an older child. Immediately after birth, a full bladder can be percussed before the baby's first urination. Subsequently, the best time to percuss the bladder is within an hour after feeding. A bladder that can be percussed at all times is abnormal. A distended bladder may be produced by structural abnormalities of the urethra, bladder neck obstruction, or neurological abnormalities of emptying. Occasionally, a persistently full bladder is the first clue to spinal cord pathology. The open bladder may be seen if there is a defect of the abdominal wall, such as extrophy.

The male's penis is inspected for normality of the glans, urethral opening, prepuce, and shaft. The normal length of the penis is 3.6 ± .7 cm from the pubic bone to the tip of the glans. The foreskin over the glans is stretched back to observe the urethral opening. When possible, the stream of urination should be observed from the side. (All healthy full-term newborns urinate within the first 24 hours of life [Clark, 1977]: failure to urinate within this length of time should be viewed with concern.) Normally, it is difficult to pull back the foreskin: this does not indicate pathological phimosis. The recently circumcised penis should be carefully inspected for inflammation of the incision, edema, or excessive bleeding; these are the most common complications of this ubiquitous cosmetic surgery.

The relationship of the urethral opening to the glans and shaft is noted carefully. An opening on the ventral penile surface is called a *hypospadias* (this finding precludes circumcision because the foreskin may be needed for subsequent reconstructive surgery). It is often associated with ventral penile bowing, termed a *chordee*. A urethral opening on the dorsal glans or shaft is called an *epispadias*. Urine streaming from other areas of the perineum or abdomen implies a fistulous tract. A constantly erect penis (*priapism*) is abnormal.

The scrotum is inspected for its size and rugation. The full-term male newborn should have a fully rugated scrotum with brownish pigmentation. The testes are palpated. At least one testis should be present below the inguinal canal at full-term gestation. (Stimulation of the scrotum or inner upper thigh activates the cremasteric reflex, which abruptly retracts the testes up the canal: warm your hands!) In the premature infant, the testes may not be palpable, or may only be found high in the canal. If the scrotum appears large or stretched, a flashlight is applied to the sac to determine its lucency. A varicocele, inguinal hernia, or hydrocele can be detected in this manner. Ecchmyoses and edema of the scrotum may be present after breech delivery (see also Chapter 12).

In the female newborn, the external genitalia (labia, clitoris, urethral opening, and external vaginal vault) are inspected. In the full-term female, the labia majora should completely cover the labia minora. The less mature the infant, the more exposed are the labia minora. After the examiner spreads the labia, a mucoid discharge is often seen. Less frequently, a small amount of blood may be observed. This is normal, although parents may be upset. The size and shape of the clitoris should be regarded. Note that the clitoris may appear relatively large in the full-term and pre-term neonate. Hymenal tags may be present normally, and may be large enough to alarm the observant parent.

If the external genitalia of the newborn appear ambiguous as to sexual identity, if there are abnormal openings in the perineum, or if the testes are not palpable, the abdomen and groin must be carefully repalpated for masses. In such instances, a rectal exam is very informative to note the presence of the uterus and to further locate gonads. More complete endocrinological, radiological, and genetic evaluations are required in these circumstances. The parents should be informed of uncertainty in sex assignment.

LITERATURE CITED

Clark, D. A. 1977. Voiding and stooling times in the newborn. Pediatrics. 60:457.
Perlman, M., and J. Williams. 1976. Detection of renal anomalies by abdominal palpation in newborn infants. Br. Med. J. 2:347.

14 / DIAGNOSTIC CONSIDERATIONS

This text presents the method of examining the newborn. Some common diagnostic considerations have been discussed where appropriate, usually as examples. Less attention has been directed toward arriving at a diagnosis; however, the physical examination is rarely done without some attempt to interpret the significance of the findings. Such an analysis in the healthy infant is often perfunctorily summed up by "within normal limits" (WNL). This abbreviation, although it is a convenient short hand, must be used with caution. Lack of attention to *all* details of the physical examination may not be very hazardous to an infant born at full-term under low-risk circumstances, but such off handedness will jeopardize the baby if he is at high risk because of obstetric factors, premature gestation, family history, or other influences.

To be thorough, the examiner must first make some estimate of gestational age and then some judgment about the competency of the neonate's intrinsic homeostatic mechanisms. The patient's ability to maintain temperature stability, his respiratory rate and regularity, his heart rate and its regularity, blood pressure, and capillary filling time are all good indicators of whether the baby is homeostatically competent. If these vital signs fall within normal limits, the examiner may be confident that the infant is healthy, or, at least, that any disorders are compensated at the time of the exam.

In organizing the exam's results, it is important to relate physical findings to major events in the infant's life (such as length of time since delivery or the onset of feeding). A certain amount of vital sign instability is normal within the first minutes of life, but is distinctly abnormal by 12 to 24 hours of age. Somnolence after feeding is usual; persistent lethargy is abnormal. As another example, respiratory distress occurring immediately after feeding in a previously well newborn suggests an aspiration rather than infectious pneumonia. Many of the physical findings in a newborn are transitory, as we have noted in earlier chapters.

Weight, length, and head circumference should be plotted against gestational age, which can be estimated from external and neurological developmental characteristics as described in Chapter 2. These plots can be conveniently done on the widely available growth grids from Denver, which has an elevation of 5,000 feet (Lubchenco et al., 1963), or on those from Montreal, which is at sea level (Usher and McLean, 1969). These charts present expected norms for fetal growth. Such graphic analyses allow the examiner to decide if the infant is pre-term, full-term, or post-term, and whether instrauterine growth was adequate. Both graphs are quite comparable until the 37th week of neonate age. Beyond this time the Denver grid begins to underestimate usual intrauterine growth potential at sea level. The examiner should check to see which standards his nursery uses. All nurseries should have one of these (or some other graph) available.

If the infant is short and/or light for gestational age the examiner must determine the reason. Specific causes for intrauterine growth failure are too numerous to permit categorization here; however, four general, basic reasons for poor fetal growth should be mentioned. Fetal growth may be depressed by *impaired maternal uterine blood supply, diminished genetic growth potential, intrauterine competition for nutrients,* or *environmental agents* (either chemical or infectious) that may depress cell growth or cause cell death. In making distinctions among these, it is useful to know the weight and quality of the placenta. However, it must be realized that a placenta may be small for the same reason that the baby is small, rather than being the primary cause for growth retardation. Further insights into the placenta's utility in neonatal diagnosis can be found in the text by Gruenwald (Gruenwald, 1975).

If an infant has loose skin and appears thin for his length, he may have consumed subcutaneous fat stores during an acute period of intrauterine malnutrition; therefore, the insult probably occurred after some fat storage had been accumulated, and this information crudely dates the deprivation to the third trimester.

The infant who is large-for-dates (above 97th percentile) is seen less frequently than is the small-for-dates infant. The most common situation is that of the large infant born to large parents, but there are disorders that result in an unusually high frequency of large-for-dates babies. The infant born to a diabetic mother, herself without significant vascular disease, is frequently overly large. You must be concerned with this possiblity in all "overgrown" newborns. In the presence of severe maternal vascular disease, the infant of a diabetic may actually be growth retarded, rather than too large. The details of the maternal history should make this clear. More infrequently, a large-for-dates infant with cyanosis is found to have transposition of the great vessels. Knowing these associations and the attendant pathophysiology will be a great aid in interpreting the physical findings.

So far we have attempted to determine if the infant is profoundly sick or well, and whether growth is appropriate for gestational age; such determinations are at the base of the diagnostic pyramid.

Next comes the important step of organizing pertinent physical findings in such a way that patterns become apparent. There is much to be said for the problem-oriented approach to recording observations. If clearly documented by supportive positive and negative findings, problem lists are very useful in developing an orderly approach to the newborn diagnosis. The examiner should guard against poorly planned or disorganized lists, since these may obscure diagnostic logic by fragmenting suspected disorders into a distracting number of isolated observations.

An attempt should be made to link all the abnormal findings with some common cause. Implicit in this step is an assumption that there is some focal process that impinges on each of the observedly disordered systems.

COMMONLY SEEN PROBLEMS
OF THE NURSERY AND DELIVERY ROOM

In the following section we consider examples of problems seen commonly in the nursery or delivery room. Since the intent of this book is to teach the skills needed for physical examination, no attempt is made to indicate the appropriate laboratory evaluations, or all historically important antecedents. These considerations properly belong in textbooks of pediatrics and newborn medicine, several of which are noted as general references at this chapter's end.

Our illustrative cases have been chosen to emphasize the analysis that can be performed on information obtained from the physical examination. Nursing observations of infant behavior and feeding patterns are available in all nurseries and can be included in the analytical process. Each case is presented with a standardized array of information, which should be available in most babies' hospital records.

The problem of diagnostic fragmentation can be illustrated by considering the problem of the full-term newborn noted to be pale on admission to the nursery:

Case 1

Male	Birth weight = 3500 g
Age = 12 hr	Apgar scores = 7(1') & 9(5')
EGA = 39 wk	Length = 52 cm
Dubowitz score = 40 wk	O.F.C. = 34 cm
RR = 40/min	BP = 48 torr (systolic)
PR = 140/min	

Physical examination at this time (12 hours of age) reveals a yellowish color in the mucous membranes of the mouth. The skin is visibly jaundiced over the upper chest. Palpation of the abdomen finds a sharp liver edge palpable

3 cm below the right costal margin, and a palpable spleen tip 2 cm below the left costal margin. Two feedings have been taken without difficulty; thus, the obvious pertinent findings are pallor, early jaundice, and splenomegaly.

Individual causes for jaundice are legion. Splenomegaly may be caused by many of the same entities.

Finally, pallor alone may be caused by anemia for any reason, or by peripheral vascular hypoperfusion due to dozens of entities.

The problem in this instance becomes somewhat easier as the examiner considers the whole picture. The baby is of full-term gestation and, at present, in no respiratory or cardiovascular distress. He is very recently born, so, in the absence of acute distress, we look to fetal life for the problem's onset. Although jaundice may be caused by decreased liver clearance or by increased production of bilirubin, the latter is most likely to produce early onset icterus. The placenta provides a record of fetal existence. In this case it was saved by the alert obstetrician. Its weight of 630 g suggests that it is larger than usual. Large placentas may be associated with intrauterine hemolysis or infection. The latter often causes small-for-dates babies, which this particular infant is not. Therefore, although this case cannot be differentiated by physical exam alone, a likely diagnosis is *isoimmune hemolytic disease*, easily confirmed by appropriate lab tests.

Case 2

Male	Birth weight = 3300 g
EGA = 40 wk	Apgar scores = 6(1') & 7(5')
Age = 23 hr	Length = 50 cm
Dubowitz = 40 wk	O.F.C. = 32 cm
RR = 56/min	BP = 76/40 torr
PR = 140/min	

The second case is a male infant whose face appears to be flat and whose tongue is large. The palpebral fissures are prominently slanted and the inner epicanthal folds are exaggerated. The irides are speckled. The hands look short, with stubby fingers. A single palmar crease traverses each palm. Neurological examination reveals the baby to be markedly hypotonic. There is a prominent systolic murmur along the left sternal border, accompanied by a heave. The rest of the examination is normal, with the exception of mottling of the unexposed extremities.

This baby's problem list reads:

1. cardiac abnormality (precordial heave, murmur, wide pulse pressure);
2. generalized hypotonia and small head (microcephaly); and
3. wide spread dysmorphic features involving the face, eyes, tongue, hands, and feet.

There is no history of perinatal drugs or asphyxia to account for the poor muscle tone. Temperature regulation and heart and respiratory rates are normal. The presence of widely distributed abnormalities suggests that a major part of the infant's problem occurred during embryogenesis. A low placental weight might also have been found in this case. It is likely that the prominent cardiovascular and neurological findings are part of an overall generalized abnormality, in this instance, one of the chromosonal trisomy, *Down's syndrome*. While the examiner may not be at all familiar with the cause for this infant's developmental abnormalities, he should at least recognize that the infant has a dysmorphic syndrome and consult an appropriate text (Smith, 1970). Careful, accurate recording of physical findings will frequently lead directly to an accurate diagnosis in such instances.

Case 3

Female	Birth weight = 2850 g
Age = 24 hr	Apgar scores = 4(1') & 7(5')
Dubowitz = 38 wk	Length = 49 cm
RR = 50/min	O.F.C. = 33.5 cm
Pr = 150/min	BP = 58/30 torr

The nurses note that this infant has fed poorly and had one episode of apnea with cyanosis. On examination the baby is lethargic and has jaundice, which can be traced from the face onto the upper chest. This baby has a metabolic derangement of such severity that her homeostatic mechanisms have begun to fail: she is obviously sick! But why? A common and quite serious cause for these findings is *bacterial sepsis*; however, the same findings are present with low blood sugar of many origins, the many varieties of metabolic acidosis, and so on ad infinitum. The choice between disorders is aided by appropriately chosen laboratory tests and careful review of the perinatal history. It is imperative that the physical exam be meticulous in the search for localized sites of infection. These sites include the umbilicus (inflammation), the skin (pustules), a dermal sinus over the spinal cord, painful joints, and the ears (for otitis media). Furthermore, since this infant is unstable, you must be especially alert to such measures of cardiac function as blood pressure, heart rate, and capillary filling time. This type of infant clearly deserves close vital sign monitoring, and careful, continuous observation while you search for the correct diagnosis.

Case 4

Female	Birth weight = 2800 g
EGA = 40 wk	Apgar scores = 7(1') & 8(5')
Age = 1 hr	Length = 47 cm
Dubowitz = 38 wk	O.F.C. not obtained
RR = 80/min	BP = 40/20 torr
PR = 180/min	

This baby is called to your attention because of pallor and tachypnea. Examination reveals that the baby's heart rate is rapid, her capillary filling time is 4 seconds, and her blood pressure is low normal. She is quiet but alert (State A-1), with slight nasal flaring, but no other signs of respiratory distress (Silverman score = 1). These physical findings suggest that the problem is acute and probably related to diminished tissue oxygenation. Such findings can be seen in anemia, or as a result of other, more unusual causes of decreased blood oxygen-carrying capacity. A "pure" anemia manifested so early in life is likely due to fetal hemolytic disease and is chronic; thus, it is usually accompanied by an enlarged spleen and/or liver.

Such is not the case here (in contrast to Case 1). Low oxygen-carrying capacity can also be seen in infants with acute blood loss occurring at or near the time of birth. The neonate's usual response to acute blood loss is increased peripheral vascular resistance, which decreases perfusion to the skin, in order to maintain blood flow to the brain and myocardium. The physical manifestations of such a redistribution are a prolonged capillary filling time, visible pallor, tachycardia, and tachypnea. These infants lie quietly and appear apprehensive. As with most of our examples, the correct diagnosis will be determined by careful physical examination coupled with knowledge of the inter-relationships among the physical findings and by narrowing diagnostic possibilities and efficiently recommending further studies. Placental findings might be helpful here as well. Again, pertinent laboratory evaluation of both mother and child will establish an accurate diagnosis. In this case, prompt diagnosis and expert intervention is mandatory.

Case 5

Male	Birth weight = 3700 g
EGA = 41 wk	Apgar scores = 6(1′) & 8(5′)
Age = 36 hr	Length = 50.5 cm
Dubowitz = 40 wk	O.F.C. = 35 cm
RR = 80/min	BP = 60 torr
PR = 140/min	

On physical examination the infant is noted to be both cyanotic and greyish in color. The Silverman score is 3. The baby is quiet, and looks apprehensive, but struggles as he is manipulated during the exam. Auscultation reveals a clear chest. Palpation finds generally diminished pulses.

There are primary respiratory, cardiac, and neurological causes of cyanosis. The physical examination will help differentiate among them. The modest amount of respiratory distress, evidenced by the minimally elevated Silverman score, suggests that primary lung disease is unlikely. In infants with neurological causes for cyanosis, the respirations are likely to be shallow or irregular; furthermore, the infant's struggling activity suggests an appropriately functioning CNS. Generally, babies with primary heart disease have relatively good air entry, although rales may be heard with pulmonary edema. Diminished air entry, the presence of increased precordial activity, a murmur, or blood pressure differences between upper and lower limbs will point toward specific cardiac entities. Infants suffering from those cardiac lesions that make survival dependent on a patent ductus arteriosus become symptomatic around the second or third day of life, when the ductus closes. This seems to fit the time course in this case and, with the physical findings, points toward an accurate diagnosis.

Respiratory distress in the delivery room demands immediate, thoughtful evaluation. The following case is illustrative:

Case 6

Female	Birth weight = 3900 g
EGA = 40 wk	Apgar scores = 8(5′) & 6(1′)

Age = 15 min   Length not obtained
Dubowitz not obtained   O.F.C. not obtained
RR = 75/min   BP = 42 (flush) torr
PR = 160/min

The infant gasped spontaneously at 15 seconds of life, then developed severe
respiratory distress (an increased Silverman score), followed by irregular
respirations. The amniotic fluid contained no meconium. Such behavior is
not characteristic of severe perinatal asphyxia, or of fetal drug depression.
Primary cardiac disease is usually well compensated during fetal life, and
often does not cause serious respiratory symptoms during the first day
of life.

The basis of this baby's problem lies in either the upper or the lower
airway. This differential can be resolved by testing her nares for patency.
Direct visualization of the larynx and posterior pharynx will eliminate the
possiblity of obstruction here.

Lower airway disease is commonly caused by a space-occupying lesion,
aspiration, pneumonia, or a developmental delay in pulmonary maturation.

Two space-occupying lesions that cause acute symptoms are *pneumothorax* and *diaphragmatic hernia*. Physical findings of unilaterally increased
resonance, decreased breath sounds, and a shifted cardiac impluse support
the former diagnosis. Transillumination is diagnostic, but this equipment is
not readily available in the delivery room. In diaphragmatic hernia, percussion may reveal a dull note over the site of the hernia. The abdomen may
be flat or even concave (scaphoid) if most of its contents lie in the chest.
Both entities require immediate expert management.

Aspiration, infectious pneumonia, and pulmonary immaturity (hyaline
membrane disease) will be diagnosed only after a comprehensive review of
the pertinent history and the laboratory, x-ray, and clinical factors.

Case 7

Female   Birth weight = 3500 g
EGA = 39 wk   Apgar scores = 7(1') & 9(5')
Age = 3 days   Length = 51 cm
RR = 40/min   O.F.C. = 33 cm
PR = 140/min   BP = 65/40 torr

The baby's temperature regulation has been normal, and her behavioral
state is A-3. She is alert and appears healthy at this time. She is being
examined for discharge. The initial physical examination on the day of birth
was less than optimal because the baby cried vigorously. When examined on
this, the second occasion, she is found to have a mass in her left flank (the
term "mass" is neutral and does not allow inference of its origin). A careful
description of the mass improves the likelihood of being correct.

First, there is its location. The abdomen is traditionally divided into
four quadrants by perpendicular vertical and horizontal lines, which
intersect at the umbilicus. The liver is the most prominent organ in the right
upper quadrant and extends just over midline on the left. The spleen is in the
left upper quadrant. The liver, stomach, spleen, and much of the small
bowel are easily mobile and superficially palpable. The location of the
baby's mass in the left flank suggests that it is probably retroperitoneal:

here, the structures are far less mobile and are only palpable on deep examination. The major structures in the retroperitoneal space are the kidneys, ureters, adrenal glands, fatty tissue, and aorta. Only the first and last structures may be felt.

Two rare malignant tumors, even more rare in the newborn, arise in this area. These are the *Wilms tumor* and the *neuroblastoma*. They must be distinguished from the more frequent developmental enlargements of the kidney and its collecting system, as well as the occasional renal or adrenal hematoma, which may follow a difficult delivery.

No mass can ever be unequivocally diagnosed by physical examination alone, but it is often possible to tell whether a mass is renal or non-renal.

The consistency is important. This infant has a rather soft, round, cystic mass that measures about 10 cm and is slightly moveable. The cystic quality suggests that the mass is renal and that it is more likely to be caused by a thin-walled hydronephrotic kidney than by a solid neoplasm such as Wilm's tumor. Polycystic disease of the kidney may produce similar findings but involves both kidneys. The consistency is firmer in the polycystic kidney because there is no urinary egress for the cystic fluid. Multicystic disease of the kidney is unilateral. its consistency is firmer than that of the hydronephrotic kidney. Clearly, your confidence in appreciating distinctions between consistencies develops only with experience.

Perhaps it would be unfair to leave this case without commenting on neuroblastomas, the other major malignancy of infancy. On palpation, these tumors are solid, firm, and fixed. In contrast to the rubbery smooth texture of the Wilms tumor, the surface texture of the neuroblastoma is rough. If a malignant tumor is seriously suspected, the number of examinations performed should be minimized to reduce chances of metastasis.

These cases should illustrate that the physical examination is most useful when it is integrated with a knowledge of developmental physiology. A careful physical examination, illuminated by the perinatal history, provides most of the information needed to point toward diagnosis. Laboratory investigations may then be efficiently directed toward answering specific questions. The examiner's data base will grow with experience and with diligent self-education through reading. Again, the novice is referred to the general references at this chapter's end as an introduction to newborn medicine.

GENERAL REFERENCES

Avery, G. B. 1975. Neonatology. J. B. Lippincott, Company, Philadelphia.

Behrman, R. 1973. Neonatology. C. V. Mosby Company, St. Louis.

Cockburn, F., and C. M. Drillien. 1974. Neonatal Medicine. Blackwell Scientific Publications, London.

Klaus, M., and A. Fanaroff. 1973. Care of the High Risk Neonate. W. B. Saunders Company, Philadelphia.

Schaffer, A., and M. E. Avery. 1977. Diseases of the Newborn. 4th Ed. W. B. Saunders Company, Philadelphia.

Smith, C. A., and N. M. Nelson. 1976. The Physiology of the Newborn Infant. 4th Ed. Charles C Thomas, Springfield, Ill.

LITERATURE CITED

Gruenwald, P. 1975. The Placenta and Its Maternal Supply Line. University Park Press, Baltimore.

Lubchenco, L. O. C. Hansman, and E. Boyd. 1963. Intrauterine growth as estimated from liveborn birth weight data at 24 to 42 weeks gestation. Pediatrics 32:793.

Smith, D. W. 1970. Recognizable Patterns of Human Malformation. W. B. Saunders Company, Philadelphia.

Usher, R., and F. McLean. 1969. Intrauterine growth of liveborn caucasian infants at sea level. Standards obtained from measurements in 7 dimensions of infants born between 25 and 44 weeks of gestation. J. Pediatr. 74:901.

Index